Go to:
Pagiel.Life

PAGIEL

A STORY OF A LIFE
- REBORN

DAVID RUSH

Marketing & Design by:
Tikvah Marketing
www.TikvahMarketing.com

PUBLISHER:Tikvah Marketing
1110 E. Main St.
Suite 305
Lebanon, OH 45036

AUTHOR: David Rush
dave@tikvahmarketing.com

1st Edition

TikvahMarketing.com

"A sculptor does not use a 'manicure set' to reduce the crude, unshapely marble to a thing of beauty.

The saw, the hammer and the chisel are cruel tools, but without them the rough stone must remain forever formless and unbeautiful.

To do His supreme work of grace within you, God will take from your heart everything you love most.

Everything you trust in will go from you. Piles of ashes will lie where your most precious treasures used to be!"

- A.W.Tozer

Chapters

Pagiel.

An unusual name; not a name I've ever heard before, yet it's a Bible name. If you've ever read the Bible from cover to cover you've seen the name, you wouldn't even need to read that much, just the book of Numbers. You probably just breezed over it like I did and didn't notice.

The Pagiel of the Bible is a prince, a man chosen to stand before God and make a significant offering to God for his people. This Pagiel, the Pagiel of our book might be just a tall skinny fifteen-year-old boy, but he's no ordinary boy.

If you ever meet Pagiel, you'll notice something different right away, but you won't be sure what it is. Yes, he's goofy, as much as any teenager, maybe more than most. His quick smile and creative lyrics to a customized song will disarm you faster than you can catch it. But this Pagiel isn't ordinary, he isn't typical. A man who makes an offering to God, who stands as a prince and represents his tribe - his people, can't be ordinary.

This Pagiel is the kind that will stand face to face and look the demons of darkness directly in the eyes, and take back what has been stolen. Not because he has any great power, not even because he's especially brave, but because God has chosen him for a special purpose. Maybe that makes Pagiel a warrior. I don't know, what do you think?

But I've jumped way ahead, we need to go way back and get to know this boy. It's a difficult and sometimes tragic story, but it's a true story, a story worth telling.

Follow me, but hold my hand tightly because this story is both exciting and troubling. The realities of life can be painful, unsettling, and often unspeakable, but to disarm our demons we need to call them out. Let's take this journey together, let's face Pagiel's demons together, and maybe your demons too. Let's see what makes this ordinary, typical teenage boy anything but ordinary and typical.

Let's see what makes him a prince who has made an offering and will represent his people to God.

I
ONCE
WAS
BLIND
BUT
NOW
I
SEE

Amazing Grace

John Newton

"...through the grace of the Lord Jesus Christ we shall be saved." -Acts 15:11

Wm. Walker

1. A - maz - ing grace, how sweet the sound, That saved a wretch like me!
2. 'Twas grace that taught my heart to fear, And grace my fears re - lieved;
3. Thru man - y dangers toils and snares, I have al - read - y come;
4. When we've been there ten thousand years, Bright shining as the sun;

I once was lost but now I'm found, Was blind and now I see.
How pre - cious did that grace ap - pear The hour I first be - lieved.
'Tis grace has bro't me safe thus far, And grace will lead me home.
We've no less days to sing God's praise Than when we first be - gun.

When I was living each day with the demons of depression, I was blind. Every day I was convinced that I was ugly. Every day the demons told me I was a freak or schizophrenic or bothersome. Every day I believed it more and more. I was blind to the love of God; I was blind to the love of my own mother and father. I was blind to the truth. I was convinced that the voices were right. I was so blind I couldn't see the truth, I couldn't even imagine the truth.

But today I can see. God, through a miraculous moment, transformed my mind. He transformed my thinking. He took me, a boy who was incurably blind, and caused me to see.

Today I see clearly. I see that I am perfectly loved. I am not only loved by God, but I can see the love of my mother and father and so many others.

The Bible says that 'For God so loved the world, that He gave his one and only Son, that whoever believes in Him should not perish, but have eternal life.' But I thought He only loved the world, as a big group, I was blind to the fact that He loves me personally. I couldn't believe that He could love just me.

Today my eyes are open to the truth. Today I do not believe the lies that were whispered in my ears. I am not a freak or schizophrenic or bother-some. Today my eyes are open to the truth that you are loved too.

God changed my life. God opened my eyes. I was blind but God caused me to see. Let me tell you my story.

My name is Pagiel Griffith; I just turned 16 years old and it's another beautiful year to be alive. This story is a little bit about me, but I want it to be about God because of what He's done to me in life, even before I was born.   I would love to share with you about the miracles of my life, even the miracle that happened in our barn.

I would like to discuss with everyone how God saved me; how God saved me with His hand, in my attempt at suicide.

On the night of October 8th, 2017, I tried to kill myself. I went into the barn and I took a .38 revolver, and I shot myself in the head. But God placed His hand on the barrel, moved it to just the right spot, so that now - the only thing I have to deal with is physical blindness. I no longer have to deal with the real blindness that I had before. Depression and the darkness and what the de-mons had done to me had blinded me to the point of death.

- This is Pagiel's story. . .

BROKENNESS

By: David Rush

Today I had an opportunity to sit down and listen to Bethany and Pagiel's life stories, from before his birth to today. There were times of laughter, and many times of tears. Pagiel is sixteen at the time of this writing, a little over a year since the day he pulled the trigger, blowing a hole through the front of his skull. His thin pale face, beautifully restored, is soft and smooth. He sits beside his mom, listening quietly as she tries to unroll the early years of his life. His one blue eye, although totally blind, follows the conversation between his mother and me. The other, mostly closed, hides the blood-red cavern that once held his other eyeball.

There is a Godly mixture of peace and intensity in Bethany's gray-blue eyes as she painfully reveals the horrors and reality of her own childhood. Her friendly face, with her short brown hair pulled behind her ears, hints at the hidden anguish of the years, including the recent events that have undoubtedly taken a toll on her countenance.

Pagiel comes from a broken home, as so many do. His story might start out very much like your own story. His mother has a history of very young childhood rape, and later, broken relationships with men that go back to her earliest teenage years. Pagiel's dad comes from a divorced home as well.

The relationship between Pagiel's mom and dad was one of passionate love and equally passionate fights. It was a passion, I suppose, that truly belonged to God, but the relationship was doomed long before Pagiel entered the world. At the time of Pagiel's conception however, Joseph and Bethany were doing well, and still together.

Bethany's parents were equally broken. Her father died from suicide and her mother's life revolved around drug and alcohol addiction. The only adults in Bethany's childhood were emotionally absent and parental guidance was in the form of negligence. Fortunately the chemical addictions of her blood relatives were not passed down to Bethany. Certainly she experimented with all of it: drugs, alcohol, sex, and more sins than need to be described here. But neither addiction nor substance abuse took hold.

As a three-year-old toddler, pre-teen boys were violating Bethany's tiny body daily and weekly. By age four, her stepfather would begin to consistently and painfully invade her between her thin young legs, leaving physical and mental scars that would last a lifetime. She was a child growing up in dreadful shadows.

Later, a revolving door of men in Bethany's young life was her way of searching for the love she'd never had. By the time she was fourteen she was in a "serious" relationship with a boy, and by fifteen she was facing a brutal, forced, and illegal abortion.

Bethany's birth mother had threatened to beat the baby to death while still in the womb if Bethany didn't abort it. Her father agreed to pay for the abortion as a replacement for future Christmas and birthday gifts. As Bethany slowly unveils her deepest secrets, her tears and pursed lips reveal the torment she still endures from the guilt of having murdered her unborn daughter so many years ago.

More than a decade later, at twenty-six years old, Bethany went to the doctor, convinced she had cancer or some other life-threatening disease. The doctor asked if she was pregnant. "Of course not," she replied with frustration. She was offended with the doctor for ignoring what she thought was the obvious fact of a serious and deadly cancer consuming her body. The doctor sent her home with instructions to do a pregnancy test in the morning.

"My mom, of all people, had just bought me a Bible," Bethany explained, "one of those with the burgundy leather cover with my name in the corner embossed in gold; the kind everyone in the south seems to have." In a whirlwind of emotions, she opened the Bible and saw the name "Pagiel" standing out boldly to her eyes. She slammed the Bible back down. She looked to Joseph, Pagiel's dad, and simply stated, "I'm having a baby, it will be a boy, and his name will be Pagiel."

The next morning she did a pregnancy test at home. Actually, she took multiple tests, just to be sure. She had to face the fact that her doctor had been right. . . The test was positive.

Bethany never expected pregnancy was possible. The results from the years of early childhood penetrative trauma and the effects of the careless abortion had left her, she thought, incapable of pregnancy. She'd had an endless string of relationships with men that all could have impregnated her, but never did.

Now, somehow, regardless of her past, God had other plans and she had become pregnant.

Joseph wasn't so sure about the name, but she was convinced.

When Pagiel was born he had a birthmark shaped like the letter "P" on his thigh; he still does. (As an interesting side note: Pagiel's dad's middle name is Whetsell, and he has a "W" birthmark on his shoulder.)

Pagiel was born very healthy and happy but the marriage between mom and dad had crashed. Betraying her, Bethany's best friend of seventeen years was now sleeping in what had been Bethany's place in bed and Bethany had to find a new home. Husbandless and friendless, Bethany took Pagiel and began a bitter and hate-filled journey. She was angry with Joseph, angry with her long-time best friend, and was slowly, intentionally and sinfully turning further away from any hope of knowing God.

EARLY YEARS

By: David Rush

When Pagiel was old enough to start school, many things had changed in his life. By this time, Bethany had bounced between various relationships and Pagiel was growing up in a very unsteady world.

Custody battles between parents were in full

swing. The physical distance of nearly four hours between individual parents meant long hours on the roads every other week. Court battles ensued. Dad threatened to pick up Pagiel with the police, but he never actually did, thank God.

Bethany and Pagiel moved in with Bethany's dying mom to care for her. Pagiel was tossed between dad, mom, and even Bethany's new husband or boyfriend's home.

The courts threatened to send a guardian to come live in the house. They wanted a psychologist to interview Pagiel. Little Pagiel wanted to live anywhere they would let him play video games. Bethany saw that her son was being torn in two.

I listened as Bethany sat back on her old, worn victorian second-hand couch and recounted the time she had written a letter to her attorney, with memories of the Bible story of Solomon in her head. The story of Solomon was of a woman who argued with another woman about the rights to a single baby and King Solomon took up a sword to slice the baby in two so that each of the two mothers could have one half of the baby. In the Bible story, the true mother cried out, "Oh, my lord, give her the living child, and in no way kill him!"

King Solomon said, "Give her the living child, and definitely do not kill him. She is his mother."

I watched emotionally as tears welled up in Bethany's eyes as she choked on her words in this prodigious memory. She had told the attorney, "we're ripping my baby in half, so he can have him."

She paused to compose herself before continuing. "I went caving by myself that night (you're not supposed to do that). I just needed time alone, by myself." It was a long night of silence in the terrifying and yet massive protective safety of the cave. Thoughts of guilt, pain, love and hatred flooded her confused mind. Nothing in her world was right; everything had come unraveled at the loss of her son. Bethany continued, "In the morning I came home and took my caving helmet off and threw it on the couch."

Suddenly, there were shrieking screams of torment unleashed through her ears and her home. Bethany thought, what is that god-awful noise?

Bethany cried, "I realized, it was me, wailing! The culmination of every pain I had ever felt in my entire life was boiling up from inside of me. Nothing in the past had ever broken me until this point, nothing."

"I had just lost my child!" she cried.

I sat watching Pagiel and Bethany in their comfortable old trailer-house. Pagiel, uncharacteristically expressionless, sat beside his mother. Silence filled the paneling-lined walls of the room as Bethany re-lived that enormous moment. Words couldn't satisfy. Dead air deafened my ears with the visible pain in Bethany's heart as she shared this emotional memory she had believed, at the time, would never heal.

"And then I took him to meet his dad, shortly thereafter," Bethany continued in a pained, quickened, and somber voice, "and he had on a blue tee-shirt and I took him to I-HOP. He had sweet tea and he was super excited to leave and go live with his dad. And that was fair, 'cause he loves us both equally, and he should, and I knew he should have permission to do that. And I watched them drive away." Then, with brokenness in her voice she added, "and then I just shut down - for a long time."

Again, silence fueled by the memory of her heart - her child, ripped from her breasts.

LITTLE
THINGS
MEAN
A
LOT

By: David Rush

Pagiel was a cute boy, the kind with longish sandy-blond hair that you just want to tousle as you walk by. He was so incredibly sweet and innocent, yet already building dangerous walls of emotional protection around himself.

Pagiel recounted his memories of those early days between mom and dad, "I remember whenever I would get in the car to go back to my dad's.

I wanted to know, a little too much, the bad things about mom." Pagiel was searching for anything that would justify his own hurting heart at the time. He fished for reasons to love his dad more. Somehow he needed to know it was okay to be with his dad. So dad would talk about all the bad things.

"I even started to exaggerate things at home, (living at Gramma's who had passed by this time). I would make too big of a deal of the problems where we lived and would stretch the truth. I would say things like, 'there were holes in the floor,' or 'we didn't have AC,' and 'there was black mold everywhere.' None of it was true. But some-thing in me really wanted to make it okay that I wanted to leave that place."

Pagiel began to fuel the problem between his mom and dad, trying to find ways to make what dad was saying to be true. He was making a childish attempt to convince himself, his dad, or anyone who would listen to him that it was a bad place.

I looked on as Pagiel sat on the cream colored couch with his hands in the pockets of his black hoodie, recounting some of those early memo-ries. "I was kind of, without even knowing it, trying to brainwash myself to believe that this was a bad place, that I hated this place. But in reality, I remembered good memories of those times. I remembered we would have festivals there some-times. I remembered I would run free on the farm that we lived on. I remembered the people and friends who lived there. I remembered I had a little canoe there and I would canoe around the pond, go fishing, go exploring. I remembered loving memories there too."

I was grateful that the two of them, sitting across the couch from each other, were so comfortable being honest and open with me. We all have those forgotten memories we would prefer were left forgotten. But, sometimes these things need to be discussed in the open. One such thing was Pagiel's growing addiction to video games as early as seven and eight years old. I suppose it was little Pagiel's way of escaping the unfair noise of his unsettling life.

Light came to Pagiel's face as he recounted one such memory. "I had an obsession, or a better word, honestly, 'addiction' to video games. I remember a couple of times that I literally sat there just playing games all day to the point where I knew I had to pee. I knew I had to go, but I would just sit there and rock and bounce my leg until literally I just wet myself - all over the place."

Mom sat silently, lips tight, looking from Pagiel and back to me, nodding her head. Finally, she spoke up again, "We had air conditioning in the house, we had window units, but I desperately wanted Pagiel to go outside. I would not leave them on, and we would both go outside during the day. I thought that was important. I saw the propensity for addiction to video games when he was very young."

"I remember I took his large video game console away - for life," Bethany said, "he could play games at people's houses, but he would never have another one in my home." Then she paused, and added, "I think that definitely did not help."

The removal of the game console created a sore point between mom and Pagiel that began opening a schism that would last nearly a decade.

Pagiel added, "To be honest with my young selfish mind, that was a big reason I wanted to move to Daddy and Nonny's." (Nonny is what he calls his stepmom). "I remember begging mom to let me go to Daddy. It was anger fueled. I would loudly and vehemently demand she let me go to Daddy's."

Pagiel explained, "It was like Nonny and Daddy were on one side with my hand in their arms, and mom on the other side with my other hand in her arms and they all pulled and they were ripping me apart."

At Dad's, Pagiel had an XBox 360 that he wouldn't just play sunup to sundown - he would play past that. "I wouldn't even eat meals when I was alone in the house," Pagiel said, "I would get hungry, even annoyed that I had to be hungry. I might grab some snack foods and set it beside me while I played my XBox."

So, unquestionably, there was significant tension in both of the homes. Mom and Dad were playing tug-of-war with Pagiel. Pagiel was fighting for his rights to video games, assumably to block out the troubles of life. Mom had different men in the home at various times, or dating regularly; probably more men than can be remembered.

However, overall, little sandy-haired Pagiel could be described as: always respectful, always good, and always joyful. For the most part, on the outside, Pagiel had a cute smile, was very polite, and loved by everyone.

Pagiel felt Mom was too strict. "Mom had rules, and at Daddy and Nonny's I had freedom. I felt free at Dad's."

"I remember his first real anger; I think this was just natural," Bethany recalled. We had started homeschooling and, of course, I was going to do everything perfect," she chuckled, rolling her eyes. "So we had this horrible schedule; every hour was scheduled. I had researched age appropriate chores. I did it all…" She paused, laughing at herself. "This is every homeschooler's first year, unless you're a better mother than me - and thank God they do exist!"

"It was after school, and he turns around in the kitchen, and he balls up his little fist, and he's shaking and he's purple. His veins were popping out, and he says, 'You ask too much of meeeee,' stretching the sound of his little-boy voice to communicate his fierce anger.

"I remember standing there looking at this tiny human and I think, 'Who is this?' and 'I kind of want to punch you in the face right now,' Bethany said, "At first I sent him to his room. I needed a minute. Then, I decided what to do. I went in there and said, 'Pagiel, I'm sorry you feel that way (which is not an authentic apology, but it's the one he got). Tomorrow you will be Mom, and I will be Pagiel.' It was Saturday, so, I laid in bed and watched cartoons while he did laundry and swept. By noon he was ready to be Pagiel again."

This little incident is somewhat funny, but it's a symptom of a child's pain growing under the surface, unnoticed and unchecked. These bursts of anger would continue to grow in frequency and gain energy through the years.

DARKNESS

<u>Pagiel Speaking</u>

I remember at one point, I started getting into Goth stuff. I liked being Goth. I was sort of introduced to it a little earlier, but this was the point in my life where I wanted to be Goth."

I wanted to wear all black. I wanted to have some chains, bracers, some spikes, some big tall boots or straight black Converses that were $220."

All of my life, I was obsessed with spooky stuff. When I was six I asked Mom to decorate my room like Halloween. I watched 'The Nightmare Before Christmas' all the time - ALL THE TIME! I just could never put it down.

I definitely had an attraction to the hauntyness side of death - the spiritual aspect of death. I remember when I wanted to be Goth and I wanted Daddy and Nonny to take me to Hot Topic to buy me black Goth clothes. Daddy said that Goth was Satanic. I don't believe wearing black means I worship Satan, but I do believe now that my obsession with Goth and death and black was a work of the devil - that is Satan.

I was so wrapped up in this Goth thing and I wanted it so, so bad. It did eventually come to a point where Daddy and Nonny took me to 'Hot Topic' to buy black clothes.

I was watching Teen Titans all the time. There was one teen member on it, her name was Raven. She was dark; she was brooding, but what I really liked is, she was magical. She had magic with her. I was trying to be Christian at the time. But I can see now I was not. My eyes were not open yet.

I remember even one night sitting up and praying to God out loud, 'God, please send me a magic spell book or something, something, something, to give me magic powers.'

I remember going around the app store and I typed in 'Witch games' and I remember finding 'Wiccan Spell App'. If you don't know, Wiccanery is a type of witchcraft; it's painted as light-full. It looks like you are in control of your own universe. You're doing good by taking control. It parallels with Satanism when you look into it.

I remember downloading this app. This wasn't a good moment.

I was reading it constantly. I hadn't done anything yet, but I was learning everything. I convinced myself I was Wiccan. I wanted everything to make me 'be Wiccan.' I remember one time, sitting on the bleachers at school with an ink sharpie and I drew a pentagram. I just loved it, and I didn't know why.

After awhile I decided, If I was a Wiccan witch, it was time to cast my first spell. Let me tell you, this was my first and my last. I cast a spell that was supposed to make it rain. I was alone. I picked a day with a forecast without any clouds or chance of rain. I did the spell, and thunder came, then rain came from the distance.

At first I was in awe. I realized, 'I did this!' Then something about that moment frightened me. I realized, 'This is dark.' I didn't know why.

I ran straight to my room, deleted my app. It really scared me.

I remember talking to a friend at school about it. I remember one time when a boy in science class saw me reading a book in my free time. I was always reading a lot about witches, the history of witches, witchcraft, Salem, things like that. This boy said, 'Dude, you know witches aren't real, right?' I said, 'Yes they are.' We went back and forth. Finally I said, 'well, I am one.' He looked confused, like, 'Are you serious?'

I explained what I had done. 'Ya, I'm a witch, well I'm a Wiccan, I can do things. I can do spells. I can control things - and it works, buddy! I can make it rain.' With my friends, I would tell them to keep it secret.

VAMPIRES

Pagiel Speaking

By the time I was ten or eleven I had started talking to a girl, well, a woman, online. (She was in her mid-twenties. Later I would understand that she was a sexual predator). She said she was a vampire. I was already interested in vampires. I read books about vampires and watched movies about vampires. She convinced me that vampires are not myths, they are real, and that she was one.

About this time I was able to buy some real looking fangs. Not the cheap mouthpiece type, but the actual real fangs that can be glued to your canines. After awhile, that's all she and I would talk about online. Then I remember I started to wonder if I was a vampire as well. She ran me through a list of questions that verified that I was, in fact, a vampire. I believed her. I wanted to be a vampire, and I started to think like a vampire.

By the time I was twelve I was becoming obsessed with vampire stuff.

I also began to have an obsession with the moon. I would stare at the moon for hours, worshiping it as my symbol. If there was a special moon, a full moon, or especially a blood moon, I would get a surge of energy or power. I would stay out all night whenever I could. It really started taking ahold of me.

She (the woman) believed she was reincarnated many times and has always been a vampire, in all of her lives. Her father was Vlad the Impaler. I even came to believe that I was her son, the grandson of Vlad the Impaler. For me it wasn't just fantasy games, it was real. I obsessed about it. I became convinced that he was actually good, but in truth Vlad the Impaler was a terribly evil man. But he was my hero.

By the time I was fourteen, I was really into video games. It was my life. I was really into a game called Minecraft and I was looking around in it and found a mod for it called 'Necromancy mod'.

For a couple of days I thought it was really cool and I really wanted to add that mod. So I started researching what Necromancy is. I learned everything I could.

Necromancy is more than simply sorcery or black magic. Necromancy is the practice of communicating with the dead or raising the dead like zombies or corpses that I could control. I searched for the answers if Necromancy was good. Of course, if you look for the answer you want, you'll find it. So, I decided that Necromancy was good.

BITTERNESS AND DEMONS

By: Pagiel and Bethany

Pagiel started, "After awhile I started hating God -- openly. Something in me just started to hate. I didn't say it out loud, not much anyway. But it was something that was always on my mind - I just hated God. I felt like I was walking around wearing it on my brain - I just hated God.

At this time Bethany interjected, her thoughts racing as she recalled those days. "If you don't have discernment and wisdom as a parent (discernment is a spiritual gift), you make mistakes. If you are not saved, you cannot have it. I wasn't saved. I went through it thinking… 'it's just a phase… He'll be fine… He'll get over it.' So, if you're not saved, you don't have spiritual gifts so…

"So, I'm thinking there are spirits in the house instead of 'demons'. I was burning sage and doing all the things the world tells you to do. They were just laughing at me. I was just making my house stink.

"But if you don't have discernment, a spiritual gift… it's not that you can't bring people back from the dead, the witch in the Bible did it, he brought back Samuel. But God says, 'Not To! - Don't!'

"There's a reason warlocks and witches were put to death. It's not because God doesn't love His people, it's because these people are infecting us.

"Without discernment you don't know if you're dealing with people or with demons. We had a house full of demons - they were running amok. We'd invited demons - Satan -- into our lives, into our homes, little by little.

"If you don't know how to pray… In the few Gospels I've read it says, 'Jesus healed someone and cast out demons,' then another place it says, 'Jesus healed someone and cast out demons again.'

"Why are we not talking about this anymore? Why are we not talking about what to do or how to pray? What does this look like?

"That's supernatural weird stuff… we don't talk about stuff like that. Meanwhile, our kids are killing themselves, our husbands are killing themselves, wives are killing themselves. Suicide is up 30% and nobody is talking about demons.

"Pagiel would come tell me when he was ten and eleven years old that he would see someone or something run across his room or he would see them at the foot of his bed. I would just say, 'oh, those are just spirits, we'll find out if they're supposed to be here or not.' But we know now, they were demons!"

Pagiel added, "I've had friends over to spend the night and we would both see little 'men' running around my room. I would just say they were spirits. My friends thought it was scary. It's not like the stuff you see in movies, or gremlins or stuff like that. It's real."

DAVE'S
NOTES

To Adam he said,

"Because you have listened to your wife's voice,
  and ate from the tree,
  about which I commanded you, saying,
'You shall not eat of it,'
  the ground is cursed for your sake.
You will eat from it with much labor all the days of your life.
  It will yield thorns and thistles to you;
  and you will eat the herb of the field.
By the sweat of your face will you eat bread until you return to the ground,
  for out of it you were taken.
For you are dust,
  and to dust you shall return."

By: David Rush

It's a matter of tuning your ears to a different voice. Were Adam and Eve demon possessed? No. They listened to Satan's voice instead of God's. They had learned to listen to Him. They had just turned their ears to a different voice. This is no different.

If Pagiel, early in life, when all of this started happening, hypothetically, if he had the training or teaching or community around him, he might have been able to say, 'I'm not going to get into that Goth stuff, that just seems ungodly to me.' Or, 'I'm not going to touch that vampire stuff, because it glorifies drinking blood, which God condemns. So, obviously it's not of God and it's actually against God. I'm not going to play with that stuff, I'm not even going to touch it.' If that could have happened, he never would have gotten here.

He would already have been prayed over and Scripture would be written in his heart and he would have, at least some, discernment.

But, because it was allowed to take a hold and take control, he got used to hearing Satan's voice. Whether it was human or demonic, there were voices, people talking to him, that were influencing the decisions he made, even influencing what he thought he liked. He didn't get the desires of his heart because he didn't hear the voice of God. He'd heard only the voices that were in his home, on his TV, on the Internet, and the voices he allowed into his heart."

CUTTING
AND
STEALING

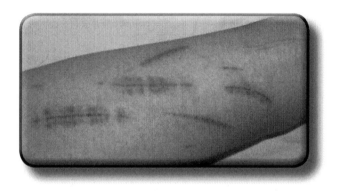

By: David Rush

Pagiel later got into stealing things, just for the thrill of it. He had been playing a video game called 'Thief'.

"I wanted to be just like Garret, the main actor of the game," Pagiel said.

It started out really small, but he started steal-ing more and more. It didn't take long before he got caught, even to the point of getting a write-up at school. Pagiel was so scared to go home that, when he got off the bus at home, he ran into the house, grabbed a backpack and some supplies and ran. He ran away. He ran eleven miles through the swamps of South Carolina. Late that night a farmer found him.

"When I got home that night, Daddy and Nonny weren't even mad at me," Pagiel recounted. "I'd never seen that man cry but, when I got home, he held me in his arms and just cried. He made me a warm bath, and made a can of ravioli for me."

The parallel of Pagiel's Dad's love in this moment compared to God's love is striking. Nearly every human struggles in shame against God, not realizing that he is waiting for us with his arms open, ready to make us a warm bath and raviolis. Read, in the Bible, Luke 15 verses 11-32. Do you see some similarities?

Pagiel's lesson in love was only temporary, he continued to slide deeper into trouble. Do you see yourself in these chapters?

By the time Pagiel was eleven years old, his grades were failing at school. Depression was settling in over his life. Nothing he ever said was right; he felt in the way and unwanted. Nobody seemed to understand him. "I began cutting myself, just to relieve the pain," Pagiel admitted. "I remember taking a shaving razor from the bathroom and pulling it apart to get a blade. From there I just started cutting myself."

He continued, "I started looking on Youtube for ways to alleviate depression. The only things

I found were Emo talks. They would talk about how cutting themselves would give them some release, as if cutting yourself would let all the badness out. For a time, it actually would feel like that. But a little cut wasn't enough after a while."

Soon, Pagiel needed more cutting, more blood. He got a knife from the kitchen at Daddy's house, along with a fancy knife sharpener, and started sharpening it even more. He actually timed himself to be certain he had sharpened it for a full two hours to make sure it was seriously sharp. He tried it on his finger to make sure it was sharp and it cut his finger easily.

He put the blade to his neck, and pressed with lots of pressure. "I remember the pressure of the blade actually hurt," he said.   Then, quickly, he pulled the knife while maintaining pressure against the blade, sliding the sharp blade across his throat, hoping to cut through the carotid arteries. Nothing happened. No blood, no death, no success. "It didn't even cut through the skin, it just left a red mark on my neck. That's how Daddy and Nonny found out."

Unquestionably, God miraculously spared Pagiel's life

SEXUAL IDENTITY

By: David Rush

By the time he was thirteen, almost fourteen, he wasn't happy at Dad's house anymore and didn't know what he wanted. One night he simply told Daddy and Nonny he wanted to move home to Mom's. Nobody really knew what was best. Bethany had been coming and staying nearby Pagiel at a friend's house just to keep Pagiel from having to travel the eight hour drive every other weekend. One weekend, Pagiel came home with Mom and just seemed to stay. Mom moved from one living arrangement to another in the Nashville area, until moving back near her childhood home on a farm in Chickamauga, Georgia.

"It felt like I was carrying handfuls of sand," Bethany said. "Nothing worked. Everything that I touched fell apart. No matter how hard I worked, no matter how hard I loved, It didn't matter what good thing I tried to do -- it was bad. It was crazy how things were happening."

Deeper darkness was settling in over Pagiel.

When they finally moved to the farm, where they live now, there was another boy who lived not far away, about the same age, that Pagiel had known when they were much younger. They began to build a friendship and did lots of things on the farm that boys do. They discovered an old abandoned trailer-house that was no longer habitable. They worked one summer to make it their fort or clubhouse.

The other boy confessed one day that he was gay. They joked endlessly about it, but the boy was serious. Over the following weeks, Pagiel began to wonder about his own sexual orientation. The more he thought about it, the more he wondered if he himself might be gay. Earlier in his life, around ten years old, he had experienced some sexual play with another boy. Although he knew it wasn't right, he had enjoyed it. Now, his only real friend was expressing the same feelings. But Pagiel was torn. He knew he liked girls too and already had a steady and daily diet of porn and masturbation. But gay?

Slowly, Pagiel became convinced that he was at least bi-sexual. His daily rendezvous and play-time with his friend became more flirtatious. The relationship started harmless enough. Most would have considered it to be only boys experimenting and testing. But each day things went further, kissing became touching. Touching became mutual pleasuring, mutual pleasuring transitioned into oral interactions. Each meeting became more sexual until the time came that they became a couple -- openly. Boyfriend and boyfriend.

There became a cycle of break-ups, then be-coming a couple again. Then another break-up, and so on.   Finally Pagiel became fed up with the cycle and called it quits permanently. But that cycle of relationships left him lonely.

Pagiel moved deeper into video games, You-tube, and his fantasy world; and deeper into darkness.

Weeks later, in loneliness, boredom and self-loathing, he was browsing FaceBook, just fooling around, when an unexpected chat popped up on his screen. The chat was the older wom-an (now about twenty-six) who wanted to talk to Pagiel. "Hey Pagiel, can I talk to you?"

(This is the woman who was convinced she was a vampire and daughter of Vlad the Impaler and had also convinced Pagiel that, he too, was a vampire, and her son.) But, even more incredible, she wrote to confess her feelings about Pagiel, that she was in love with him.

Pagiel thought about it for a minute, and replied, "yes, me too. I love you too, Ashley."   Pagiel didn't hesitate or wait, he simply jumped in. Everything he needed to offset his loneliness and pain was right in front of him.   His sexual desires were immediately piqued. Within days his relationship with Ashley turned sexual and their days and nights were spent exploring each other physically on webcam and masturbating with each other constantly. There became no limit to their obsessions with one another.

"Well, I'm really lonely and all of a sudden there's a friend here to talk to me, and I love her too. I just fell right into it," Pagiel said.

Pagiel kept this relationship mostly hidden from his mom. But when Mom found out, she tried her best to end this unhealthy relationship, but Pagiel and Ashley had become very creative, using hidden apps and false identities to communicate, and continued their sexual exploration regularly.

The vampire beliefs grew exponentially. With her encouragement, and his renewed vampire ambitions, Pagiel started cutting himself again. This wasn't cutting because of depression; this was for the vampire nature of seeking blood.

"I remember something happened. I was walking down the road with my friend and told him about Ashley. I told him about my growing need as a vampire. He asked if I really believed I was a vampire, and I said 'yes, I am.' As a friend, he wanted to support me and help me. He became what I called a drudge. That means he becomes a vampire human slave. Later he would cut himself for me so that I could drink his blood. I got so deep into it that I bought a diabetes pen online. I looked up online that other vampires used these. I began using it on webcam with Ashley and on myself and my friend. I no longer believed I was human. My friend became jealous but continued to be my drudge.

"I was looking for every opportunity to be with Ashley and was researching ways to get to her and to live with her if there was any way possible."

Bethany didn't know the extent of any of this. She thought this was just a phase and that they were pretending the vampire thing. She thought Ashley was just a friend.

Bethany tried to get Pagiel involved in violin classes and felt that she should take him to men who would be mentors for Pagiel. Pagiel resisted. Some suggested he should be admitted to "Valley," the local mental institution. Aaron, an adult friend from church, would mentor him on Sundays and take Pagiel to church.

Pagiel hated everything his mom was trying to

do to. Everything seemed like she was tearing him away from the things he enjoyed.

"I was starting to feel more dark," Pagiel said. "I was getting more hateful and furious. But I wasn't looking for a way out of the darkness. Honestly I didn't really want out. I wanted a way out of the light. I didn't want help, I didn't want mentors or violin classes. I just wanted to be left alone. I wanted what I was into to be the reality and for everyone to just leave me alone."

Bethany chimed in, "By the summer of 2017, Pagiel was doing nothing. He wasn't doing chores, and he wasn't reading books. If I saw a glimmer of joy in him I was shocked. He was totally existing inside his own head. He was just sitting there saying 'I hate everything,' 'I hate you,' 'I'm not doing anything… anything.' Things were changing and happening very fast."

Ultimately, Bethany contacted the local police and online cyber-police about the online relationship between twenty-six year old Ashley and fourteen-year-old Pagiel. They said they would look into it, but there wasn't anything they could do. But, because of Bethany's persistence, Pagiel and Ashley lost communication. However, the result was only to drive Pagiel deeper into anger, rage, and darkness.

CHANGING PERSONALITY

By: David Rush

Pagiel turned more heavily into movies and video games to drown out the noise in his own head. He connected with a show called Mr. Robot and a star character named Elliot Alderson. He connected with Elliot because he saw himself as a computer hacker.

Mr. Robot is a story about a bad hacker who puts America into anarchy. He's a drug addict, and schizophrenic. Pagiel's years immersed in computers and video games combined with his natural intelligence had given him an uncanny knack at hacking. He always imagined himself as a "legal hacker" or a "Pen Tester". Elliot Alderson was exactly who he wanted to become. But Elliot was portrayed as a schizophrenic individual and Pagiel also began to see himself as having schizophrenia.

Pagiel went deep into emulating Elliot. He began to dress like Elliot, then to speak like him. Soon after the obsession with Elliot Alderson began, a pair of demons began to expose themselves and play good-cop, bad-cop with Pagiel. One encouraged him to be more and more like Elliot while the other tantalized him for being a freak and a schizophrenic.

Slowly, Pagiel's face even began to change. It became thin, his eyes got darker, and the area below his eyes turned an erie purple. His jawline began changing and even his voice became flat, emotionless, inflectionless. Pagiel wore a black hoodie, even during the hot Georgia months, with the hood up over his head to hide his face. The demons praised him for looking the same as Elliot.

Somehow, in Pagiel's demon-twisted mind, he believed that God was changing him. He believed that his mother hated him. Pagiel remembers being in the car one day, riding to town, when his mother turned her head to look at him and screamed in an eerie and demonic voice, "You're just a little demon!"

Looking back, Pagiel knows this was impossible, but that's what he saw and heard. He was regularly seeing and hearing things that were not of the physical world. In a sense, the world of demonic powers was becoming more real, more tangible, more acceptable to him, than the physical world around him.

Bethany remembers simply offering him something to eat and Pagiel would retort with a storm of incensed accusations.

By this time, the voices in Pagiel's head were in almost total control. He had given Satan an open door so many times and wasn't even aware of it. He had never done it intentionally. Everything he'd gotten involved in seemed innocent enough, at least at first. Bethany and Pagiel didn't have a compass to guide them between right and wrong. They had feelings, ideas, hopes and dreams, but no foundation.

CLIMAX

By: David Rush

Trying to keep Pagiel from going deeper down the rabbit hole with Ashley had become almost impossible. They had found ways to communicate on social media platforms that were not intended for chat, and used assumed names. To take the computer away from Pagiel would mean a total meltdown and there was no hope of that making things anything but worse. Bethany found out, through a friend at work, that it was possible to chat, not with a phone or tablet, but with a desktop computer, on a media platform called SoundCloud. Pagiel used SoundCloud for his "art" - at least that's what he would say.

Bethany was up in the night researching Sound-Cloud and the requirements of using an account. She found Pagiel was too young to have an account without parental permission. She knew she could at least shut down his account based on that. So, she did. She closed and deleted his account, then went to work.

When Pagiel got up in the morning, he did what he had done on so many other days: he went directly to his computer to open his SoundCloud account, not for art, but to chat with Ashley. His account was closed.

Pagiel lost it -- he exploded. This boy, once sweet and polite, was now fully possessed by demonic rage and hatred. In a blind fury he went to the abandoned trailer-house in the woods. Without even a thought or care and driven by mania and adrenaline, he began destroying the building. Furniture was lifted and smashed to the floor, cabinets were kicked in, leaving splintering wood strewn everywhere. The carpet was ripped from the floor, just to spend untamable energy. He thrust his fist and elbow through the windows, splintering old glass panes, slicing open his flesh and pouring blood on the floor and spattering on the walls. He didn't stop; he didn't even slow down.

In perverse rational, Pagiel viewed his open wound with blood and fat oozing from the filleted skin, feeling proud that he had exposed more than blood and bone but fat as well. This reinforced his self image of being muscular and fit. However, the blind reality was that he was 6'-2" tall and weighed only slightly more than 100 pounds. He was dangerously skinny and, seeing himself with fat and flesh exposed, his rage was fueled all the more.

Then, wanting to burn the dilapidated house, he went to the shed nearby and found gasoline and other liquids. Containers of fuel were dumped onto the floor but no matches were found. In his imagination, he lit and flicked burning matches on the fuel-soaked floor, but no fire would ignite.

Someone called his mom; she left work and arrived as quickly as possible. She tried to remove him from the demolished trailer-house but he refused. The altercation became physical. There wasn't any hitting, but she had to forcefully pull him out of the house. His screaming and rage never cooled.

She tried hard to force him into the car to go home, but he refused and she couldn't overpower his animal-like tantrum. He began walking, and she followed him with the car. At least he was moving toward the house. In his hatred and anger he would occasionally turn around, flip her off with both hands and shout obscenities equal to his bile wrath.

The next few days were a blur of painful silence,

outbursts of fierce anger and vulgarity. This teenage boy, once so peaceful and sweet, now had an unrecognizable personality. He became a stranger in his own home. Truly, he became a stranger to himself.

Something inside of Bethany had thought of the gun in the kitchen cabinet a few days earlier. They lived on a farm after all, so having a gun in the house was important and very common. But because of Pagiel's recent outbursts, it seemed right to hide it. The anger and rage in him had her very worried and she could neither comprehend, nor could she rule out some kind of uncontrolled violence in her son. As a precaution, she had taken the revolver and gone outside to hide the gun away in the glovebox of the car.

During these days in early October, the pair of demons no longer hid themselves from Pagiel. They no longer whispered in his ears and no longer hinted to him in his dreams. No, it was worse than that. They allowed themselves to be fully visible, fully heard, and fully controlling. They called themselves Mark and David. We will never know the reason for those particular names, but they seemed to want to identify themselves to him as "regular people." Although only visible to Pagiel, he was taunted, teased and encouraged by Mark and David day and night. Bile and bitterness were infused through their constant communication. But somehow Pagiel found kinship with them, almost a sense of acceptance.

At last, on October 7th, Pagiel had agreed to spend some time with a friend near the farm along with an adult friend of the family. Together they went to a movie and spent some time together. Bethany hoped that Pagiel would open up to somebody, and maybe he could find a ray of hope.

Bethany was on her way home that night and the adult friend had been with Pagiel but had left shortly before she got home. Pagiel had gone to bed before Bethany came home. When she arrived, she checked on him, and was relieved to see that he was sleeping, or at least pretending to sleep. Either way, he was in bed.

Pagiel, in fact, was not sleeping. He waited in his room, tortured, but believing the words of Mark and David, the demons who accompanied him day and night. "You're ugly, you're a freak, you're a schizophrenic. Just end it. You're in the way anyway. Just get it over with."

Bethany, at the other end of the house, couldn't sleep. She was reading the book, "Tuesdays With Morrie." She found some passages and thought, "I can't wait till morning, maybe Pagiel will listen to a paragraph or two." She even considered that tomorrow they would take a walk, maybe go find someone with some wisdom… anything. There was huge concern for his mental well-being, but always a ray of hope.

As she laid there, struggling for sleep, she

heard the toilet flush at the other end of the house. Somehow, that gave her some comfort. It seemed all was well for the night. She turned off her bed-side light, rolled over and went fast asleep.

Pagiel liked to write in his journal, but he was always paranoid that somebody would read his thoughts and use them against him. He had de-veloped a secret code language using a text form he called "letters of blood." This night, when he believed his mom was finally asleep, he got up, used the bathroom, then sat on his bed, writing in his journal.

As he pondered his life, he was convinced that it was over. The girl he loved would never be seen again. He believed he would have a police re-cord because the police were watching his com-puter. He believed he was a schizophrenic freak. Ending everything was becoming a necessary reality. "I want out, I'm tired of the pain, I'm tired of the struggle… I'm just tired," he thought.

He had some zip-ties he considered wrapping around his neck. He wondered if those would kill him fast enough. "No," he decided, "those would hurt too much."

Mark suggested he use a gun.

"I don't think I can do that," Pagiel said.

"We will show you how," they replied, "It's fast and painless. We can help you get used to the idea."

David came to him, taunting him, "You're thinking of suicide. You told your mom you weren't going to do it, but now you are going to do it. You're
such a liar. Well, here's a tip buddy, you obviously should at this point. You're just putting too
much on everybody. Everyone is nervous around
you. There's something wrong with you."

Frantically he started deleting everything possible on the computer. Every app, every document,
every conversation. He tried to do a factory reset
on the computer, hoping that all evidence of his
life would be erased.

Mark, the friendly, therapeutic demon, spoke
to Pagiel, "Hey, Pagiel. Calm down, slow down.
You have all night to do this. You need to do this.
This is what God has called you to do. You'll be
fine." Then Mark sat Pagiel down and explained,
"You really are going to be fine. You're going to
die tonight, but God is waiting and Ashley will be
there for you. You and Ashley will be together forever in heaven with Jesus. Or, you can be alone,
it's all up to you."

Fourteen-year-old Pagiel was ready to die. In
earlier weeks he had taken the time to research
how to correctly hold a gun to end his life. He
wanted to be sure he got it right the first time. Today might be the day that information will become
necessary.

When all the preparations were made, all evidence was destroyed, Pagiel snuck out of his room, as quietly as possible. He couldn't stand the idea of his mom catching him walking around the house and trying to explain himself. Ridiculously slow, inch-by-inch, he made his way to the kitchen. He wanted to see if the firearm was still in the cabinet.

Pagiel wasn't sure he would kill himself that night, but he wanted to be sure everything was in place. Maybe just hold the gun, get used to the feel of it in his hand. But it wasn't there. The gun was missing and Pagiel didn't know where to look. For a moment he experienced a mixture of frustration and relief.

"It's in the glovebox of the car," Mark said, "go get it.

Pagiel quietly closed the cabinet and was about to go out the door when David stopped him. "The door will squeak. Your mother will hear. Don't go that way. Go out your bedroom window. You don't want to wake your mom."

That's exactly what Pagiel did. He returned to his room. Then millimeter by millimeter, as quietly as possible, he lifted his bedroom window and gently crawled through. Once outside he tiptoed to the car and carefully lifted the door handle, moving the door open very slowly.

As he reached for the glovebox he thought," is

this really happening? Is there any hope left that I can even do this right?"

Opening the glove box he spotted the gun. He took it in his hands, feeling the heavy cold steel and knurled grip against his palm. He placed the revolver in his pocket. Then just as quietly, he closed the glove box and pushed the door tight against the body of the car, not quite fully closing it.

Pagiel made his way down to the barn, feeling more freedom outside because nobody would hear his footsteps. Not wanting to leave the gate unlatched so anyone could trace his steps, he climbed over the first gate, feeling the awkward weight of the gun in the pocket of his sweatshirt.

The barn is separated from the house by more than half a football field. In between there is a workshop and miscellaneous other sheds, trees, shrubs, and farm equipment. It would be far enough that nobody would think to look there, and certainly nobody would hear him.

He climbed over the second gate, entering the barn. The barn was familiar enough to find the light switch in the dark. The lights of the barn wouldn't be visible from the house. Switching on the old dim lights, Pagiel found his way next to a vertical wooden post near the back of the barn and sat down on a pile of old hay.

The demon, David, told him to empty the bullets. Having been in farm country much of his life, Pagiel had experience with handguns. He opened the cylinder and emptied the five lead bullets into his hands. Snapping the cylinder back into the gun, David explained, "just pull the trigger; feel the weight of it in your hands."

Leaning against that century old, hand-hewn timber, Pagiel held the .38 revolver in his hands . "Click."

"Do it again," David chided. Pagiel clicked the revolver several times.

"Now, hold the revolver to your head," David instructed.

Pagiel placed the hard steel of the barrel against the softness of his right temple. "Click."

"Now put a bullet back in," David prompted.

Pagiel placed one bullet into the cylinder. Again he lifted the gun to his head. "Click"

Okay, load the rest of the bullets," David gave his last direction as Mark watched.

This time Pagiel placed the remaining four of the .38 caliber bullets into the cylinder. Then, without hesitation or continued thought, he placed the heavy barrel of the gun against his right temple. He squeezed the trigger exactly as he had a number of times already.

But this time, in a flash, a moment, a soft warm hand touched his. Something, someone touched him. The gun, almost in a surreal slow-motion, moved forward at the same moment the firing pin ignited the powder, expelling the lead from the barrel. The potentially lethal bullet passed through directly behind his right eye, the shock-wave expanding and expelling the eye from it's socket, then intersected the frontal lobe of the brain before exiting the opposite side of his skull, just behind his left eye.

Gray brain matter and blood spattered the century-old beams as Pagiel's body writhed and twisted. Bloody hand prints still remain on the wooden posts to this day. His body clung to life, even when his intention preferred it to end. His right eyeball dangled from the exploded cavity of his face. Endless darkness enshrouded his world. Screams were muted by the soft rain on the metal roof.

A few moments after, he made a conscious decision to crawl to a nearby tarp, thinking it would make less mess. He sat, then dropped to the floor, struggling against hope through the night hours. Consciousness came in short bursts, but darkness never ended.

Never again would anything be the same for Pagiel or his family.

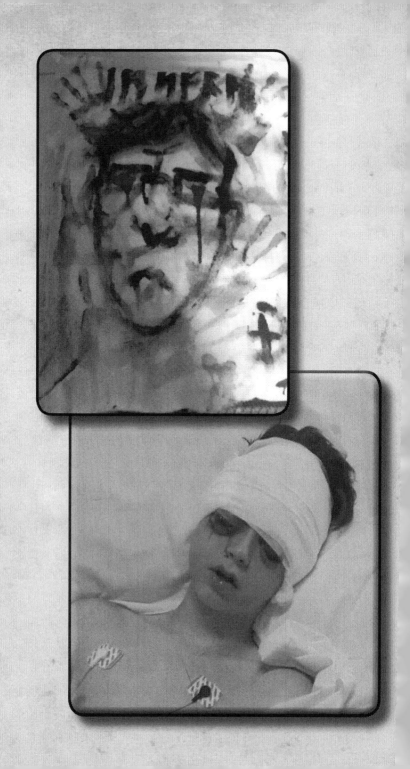

The days leading up to the attempted suicide, the demons, Mark and David, showed Pagiel images of himself, and he painted some of them.

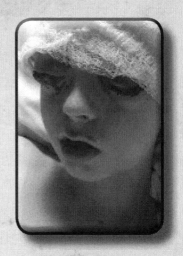

Compare his painting to the photos of Pagiel in the hospital.

The painting below is "The Shadow Man" "The shadow man was lounging on my brain," Pagiel explained, "a skeleton key was inserted where the entry wound is now and the key un-

locked a panel (where his eyesight would be removed) to look inside my head."

Again, painted shortly before the attempted suicide, but discovered days after.

The next few chapters are directly from Bethany's private journal.

It was me, crouched on a barn floor with a child who may stop breathing his gurgling breaths at any moment, his head covered in blood...moments after his suicide attempt.

When God said, "That's enough! She is MINE!!"

Then it was just God and me. I was shattered and raw and He picked up each piece to make and mend a New Creature.

I stay close now, it is safe Here.

THE
FIRST
DAY
OF
OUR
NEW
LIFE

By: Bethany

I was to wake at 8 a.m. for work. My son had been suffering from a broken heart as of late and I was keeping a close eye on him.

Parenting is difficult with an adolescent of 14 who not only needs their space but also is angry at you for trying to protect them from what shattered their heart. My protection was not enough. My mother's love was not enough. My son, whom I've always known has a Great Journey destined for him...had plans that would end his own suffering.

I woke before my alarm. I went to pour coffee and to check on Pagiel.

His bed was empty, his bedroom window wide open and it was pouring down rain.

I just knew he had run away and immediately called in to be absent from work. I quickly switched over to a different state of mind and itinerary. I scanned the room quickly for a note or other clue. Seeing nothing, I headed to the barn as I assumed the rain had encouraged him to seek shelter for the night.

A scent that was unfamiliar hit my senses before I recognized his form in the barn hall. I ran to him when I saw his body in the fetal position...curled up on a tarp. My mind did not understand what I was seeing. His head was bloody and one eye was not in its place.

I called his name... He gurgled, but answered me. I told him he was going to be OK, that I loved him and let him know I had to run for my phone to call 911.

[Bethany had to return to the house, in the rain, and find her phone.]

I did just that. When they answered, I stated the description of what my vision had captured, that I was trying to remain calm so I could relay my information without confusion.

I began giving them our address when the operator asked if he had hung himself. I told her I would have to ask him.

I asked and he replied, "yes"...but on this side of things, I know there was no way he heard the question properly.

As we waited for our rescuers to arrive... I looked around the barn. I crouched behind him as to not look at his handsome face I had known for 14 plus years, but that now seemed to confuse my mind so much. I, of course, was in shock but understood none of this at the time.

I softly but briskly rubbed his back, repeating a mantra I somehow thought would keep him alive. "Everything is going to be OK, you are so loved, nothing is EVER worth this."

Would it be OK? Did he even want to be saved? Where was the AMBULANCE? Is that the rope he used? Did he fall when it broke? Is that what happened to his eye? (It was morning, overcast and there was little light; half of his face remained in the shadows.) Had he been like this all night while I slept and knew, felt, sensed NOTHING?? Will he live until the ambulance arrives?

Finally, after calling once more and knowing I had no choice but to wait, keep him awake and repeat these imagined magical words... Off in the misty distance, I heard the sirens.

That is when I saw something more sinister than a rope. A ghastly but visible demon shared the space in the 100-year-old barn with us. And it was very pleased with itself.

UNFORGETTABLE RIDE

By: Bethany

I finally knew the rescuers had arrived. I cannot tell you the shape of their faces or if there were 3 or 5. I did rush out to meet them and made sure they knew which structure they needed to find. I cleared a path for them...warned them not to slip in the mud.

They spoke to my son. He replied... I do not remember the words.

I will never forget the face of my child when they turned him on his back onto the stretcher. The light revealed what previously was hidden in the shadows. His face did not make sense to me. None of this made sense to me.

I followed the EMTs and my son. My friend who owns the farm on which we live and rented us our home... ran to the scene as we were exiting the barn. I wondered for a moment if I wore the same expression of terror and confusion that she did.

Again, I do not remember our conversation as we walked briskly to the ambulance. I did announce I was going to ride with my son to the emergency room. An officer met me and asked me to come into the house; I followed. I probably would have acquiesced to anything requested at that moment. My body was simply going, my instinct of "Fight over Flight" was heightened.

The officer asked for my identification. Another lost conversation was had. I was asked for a plastic bag… because of the rain? I offered an umbrella. My friend said the emergency team was OK and I didn't need to find the umbrella. I know now they simply needed to distract me.

As we walked out of the house, I saw the ambulance pulling out of the drive. I felt my "Fight" transform into a crumble. Just when I thought I would fall to the earth, a voice from a rescue vehicle called out. It was a young man. He assured me Pagiel had not lost consciousness and his vitals were stable. The waters of Niagara Falls could not compare to the amount of relief washing over me.

My friend was to drive me to the hospital. I have no idea why I thought I would be allowed to drive myself. I asked her if she minded… if I was keeping her from something important. As if her world had not stopped the moment she ran to us. I had an appointment to dog sit for a client. These are the things my mind was giving me to worry about. I had no idea God was doing Big Work with me, that I was soon to live in a constant state of Faith. Faith was in the driver's seat...figuratively and literally. My friend's name is Faith. Had we not moved to her family farm earlier that year, I do not know how I would have made it through this alone.

We then made the longest ride I have ever experienced. This was longer than the time I had to evacuate Charleston, SC.; a drive that normally took 1 hour and 15 minutes developed into a 17-hour trek. But nothing could compare to the 45 minutes it took to get to my child, not knowing his condition and desperately trying to be OK, breathing into a bag and attempting to just be.

I had no idea how my path was changing beneath my feet as I took each step.

"In seasons of severe trial, the Christian has nothing on earth that he can trust and is therefore compelled to cast himself on his God alone...

"Happy storm that wrecks a man on such a rock as this! O blessed hurricane that drives the soul to God and God alone!

"There is no getting at our God sometimes because of the multitude of our friends; but when a man is so poor, so friendless, so helpless that he has nowhere else to turn, he flies into his Father's arms and is blessedly clasped therein! When he is burdened with troubles so pressing and so peculiar, that he cannot tell them to any but his God, he may be thankful for them, for he will learn more of his Lord then than at any other time."

- Charles Haddon Spurgeon

I
NEED
A
NEW
IMAGE

By: Bethany

We arrived at the hospital. I was lost. I was in a protected coating of "just go." I found the front desk in the correct entrance after going to the incorrect one. A human...the exact form escapes me...came to bring me to the Emergency Room. My son was talking. He was moving. It was as if he had just a bump on the head. Everything was going to be OK!!!

The doctor asked if I had a gun in my house. My brain was thinking in tunnel vision and I pictured where I used to keep the gun. (I myself cannot shoot but my son's father had educated him). "No" I replied, because I had moved the gun. There was no gun in my house because it was in my car! It WAS just a bump on the head. You see, shock does not allow for a spider web of thought, only snippets and bits at a time.

He asked the question in a different way as I imagine he has had unfortunate experience with these things. "Do you have a .38?" I sunk. I put my head down and my hands to the sides of my head. Yes...I did. He led me to my son to show me the entrance wound in the right temple and the exit wound in the left. My son exclaimed, "Ow! That HURTS!!" and apologized for being rude. How was this possible? This is not happening. In a busy room full of people and nurses and doctors... I felt solitary in my impending grief and terror.

My son was taken to surgery to remove his right eye. I had to call his father. We did not have a great relationship at the time and I wished that was a call I didn't have to make. I agreed to the surgery... then Faith and I were in a room with the Chaplain. I had never met him before, but I was eternally grateful for those two people at that moment. I made the call. I filled out paperwork. Faith called people that called other people. Soon...there were many people.

I do not remember how long this initial surgery was. I just remember that there was a moment when I began to lose my footing in the world. I wondered how I would do this? I needed to get out of the clothes I was wearing. They smelled of blood. The blood of my precious child's head... and other details that began to torment my senses.

As a team of loved ones came in, they asked

how they could pray. I asked for a new image. I knew now, my son was going to live. Though I had very little foresight… I knew with everything that I was, he needed me healthy and whole and present. At all times.

One of the women who was there was Sarah. She knew exactly what I needed as she had found her dear friend dead in a bathtub. She was a minister, a prophetess, an amazing woman of God. She knew how and what to pray for me. I, at this time...did not feel worthy to approach God with anything. I had caused my son to attempt to take his life. Me alone. This was completely my fault. I would be amazed if any of my prayers would be received by God.

But everyone gathered around me. They prayed with hands on me. As I waited for my son to survive… for the second time in hours… I was blessed. I not only was gifted a New Image, we were gifted a New Life.

TAKING
LIFE
5
MINUTES
AT
A
TIME

By: Bethany

My son's surgery went very well. In fact, one of the surgeons told me how polite my son was during pre-op. He never stopped talking, never lost consciousness throughout the entire process that I know of. He was sedated heavily as anyone would be after such an injury and such a surgery.

This is where my memory consists of staccato moments. My best friend was there, my Mama (one I have chosen, my biological mother passed years before), friends, my son's father and his wife, pastors… people came, supported, prayed, hugged, loved… Loved Us Big.

My son had extreme swelling and scabbing on his eye and socket. His face was swollen slightly...not as you would imagine. His eyes were the shocking part but the whole of his face simply looked childlike due to his full cheeks. He looked like a toddler again. He looked beautiful and precious. He looked like Life.

He would only wake occasionally. He would try to take off what was covering his eyes (there were no bandages on his eyes, just his head)...pick at the large scabs that basically now were his eyes. I knew when he did wake… he would be the same as he had become in the weeks prior to his attempt… tortured and angry, sad and overtaken. I was waiting on it. Mama was standing by me one of those times. I heard, "I don't want you here". I almost hit the floor. I looked at Mama and told her what my ears heard.

She corrected me as he had said he didn't want ANYONE around him. We were holding him down. He was trying to pick at his eyes. There were approximately 7 people holding him down. My guilt was waiting on him to still hate me.

I literally began to take life 5 minutes at a time. It would take hours to finish a text or a thought or an action… my son determined what was happening every 5 minutes. I held his hand through the night… he always wanted touch while in this state of medicated, healing unconsciousness.

We slept in chairs, taking shifts of three to four

hours. I never left. Everyone said I should take a walk, get some sunshine, take a real shower (I "bathed" in the sink). I kept his hands busy... On October 9th, I picked up my first book on Traumatic Brain Injury. I researched Suicide Attempt Survivors. I stayed in study, took notes, watched my child, talked to visitors, immersed myself in action.

Once, Pagiel sat up, he screamed, "Mama!!!! WAAAKE UP!!!" I was holding his hand and right beside him. I reassured him I was indeed awake and right there. He screamed again, "Mamaaaaa!!!! WAAAAAAKE UUUUP!!!!!" I realized this was a dream, a memory from moments after the bullet had entered his temple and he realized he wanted help. He realized he wanted life. This was all I needed to know. He did absolutely want to live!!! This is when I began to live again too. Five minutes at a time... I would carry him through this and he would one day not only live... but Soar.

NAKEDLY HUMAN

I had lost all vanity. I had been stripped down to a basic human, with no personal desire or want, no worries or thoughts that were self-serving or focused.

I simply wanted my child to live. I was not selfish in my desires for I felt as though I had failed him beyond all measure. It is important to note that I was not guilty or depressed either. I was very much alive in a way I had not been in years. I was no longer in shock nor did I have any strange PTSD symptoms or nightmares. But I would NOT fail my child this time.

He continued to thrive. When it was time to take him off his meds, he rested. I sat for hours awaiting the screaming and writhing of a body in excruciating pain. There was only peace and calm. He was in God's care. I asked the nurse if he should be feeling anything. She was somewhat baffled at his level of comfort. He would get pain meds before his first bath and a few doses of Tylenol for his fever or if we imagined he may have a headache. He never spoke of pain. His strong pain meds were removed from his list. He received guests and spoke to all that came.

He did however, speak with inflection after a few days. This was a huge miracle as a frontal lobe injury causes "The Flat Effect." A person with such an injury loses emotion, inflection and desires. The medical staff was amazed daily with his progress. They smiled in spite of themselves. Some of the nurses were absolutely smitten. One was an Angel. I saw her once. She spoke what was on my mind. She knew he had been taken over. I had to ask her to tell me the message God wanted her to tell me. She explained He had revealed that Pagiel had been in the darkest of places but that all would be well. I never saw her again.

Once the doctor brought up that he wished a gun had not been attainable. I simply stated that my son's father had educated him well with guns, that we lived on a large farm where everyone had guns. I did not want this to be a gun issue as it was a heart issue. However, in my heart I knew if, had he hung himself, we would be in a very different place.

I remember the very moment I surrendered to God. Pagiel had been to church and wanted to be a Christian in recent years but I had been in a slow decline over the years of being angry at God. I remember the day it began and we will visit that time another time. But for now...

There was a night that we had been moved to a real room, out of PICU… that Pagiel and I were alone for the first time. I was lying down to sleep and wondered how the night would go. Would I sleep very deep and not wake if he needed me? Would he hurt himself? Would I fail him again? It was then that I spoke directly to God… truly for the first time without being ashamed. "This is walking by faith," I boldly proclaimed, "You will take care of my son because he is Yours."

I drifted off to sleep because I had no choice. I had to sleep to care for Pagiel during the day and I had to have rest to be human. I was just that. Nakedly Human. Completely reliant on my Creator. I had not thought about bills or what would happen if I did not go to work.

I had a dear friend who would become a sister, cut all my hair off in the hospital bathroom, I did not put on makeup or see what everyone was doing on Facebook… I was being carried, comforted, held and adored. I had not grasped all this yet...but my walk in absolute faith had truly begun.

GIVE
ME
SIGHT,
IF
ONLY
A
LITTLE

By: Bethany

We had been in a regular room for a few days. Pagiel was extremely tired all the time. This is absolutely normal for Traumatic Brain Injury patients. He participated begrudgingly in PT, OT and ST.

He had a birthday where I ordered and his Stepmom picked up a tactile cake that said, "Happy Birthday" in Romanian, (the language he was learning), loads of special gifts from all that loved him and even from the hospital staff. He had a fever that day and turned 15 in a state we will never know about. His fiddle class came to his room for a private concert. Fellow students sang and played… his teacher absolutely has my heart forever for this gift. He dreamed and slept and could barely be roused. From under his sheets he would clap after every song.

His emotions were returning. We had been instructed to answer his questions honestly and our new doctor even bluntly told him he had attempted suicide by gunshot. We were to answer that he was blind and not anything hopeful. I learned that medical staff are excellent at worst case scenarios.

Once he was turning over to drift off to slumber. He seemed sad. Truly sad, not tired. He called me over and I took his hand in mine. His precious face with still swollen eyes, protruding and scabbed... turned to face me as though he was looking at me. I asked if there was anything he needed, anything I could do. He said, "Anything, Mama?"

"Yes, baby...I would do anything for you; what is it that you want or need?"

"Can you give me sight? If only a little?"

I exhaled. I cried silently as I had learned to do many years before. I gathered my voice so the tears would not be detectable.

"No... I cannot give you sight. But I can help you learn to be the very best blind guy ever. And I will be here every step of the way to love and guide and support you."

He turned and told me he loved me. And drifted to sleep.

TWO
TINY
MARKS

By: Bethany

I must fast forward as this is my experience at the time of this writing and I do not want this powerful moment to become misty and hazy the way that memories tend to do.

We have been home for 3 months. Pagiel is doing well as we have a support net that is without fail. God is in our lives each day showing us where we are to turn and what we need to do. We do not wake without knowing our days are led by absolute guidance. We have not been given a spirit of fear and we know that we have been given grace.

I went into the barn for the first time today. I have been TO the barn before, peeked inside, been all AROUND the barn, helped work cows in the barn ENTRANCE... but my aforementioned careful peeking had only given me a glimpse of the unsightly splatter of what I knew was not oil or some farm stain and indeed let me know I was not ready... not ready until today.

This day, I was sure I was ready. I was pulled to enter. God wanted to show me how only He can take a storm and grant you faith.

I was walking the dogs while Pagiel napped. I went in to see if any evil still lived there, to check my own composure, to see what, if anything might still haunt me... though I have and know others have walked the perimeter and prayed and exorcised.

The barn is 100 years old and the family that has loved this farm for over 50 of that still need to love it. It is just a building and the memories it houses do not make the wood dimmer or brighter. It is a barn. A beautiful old structure that I am quite sure has housed death before… it must represent life somehow as well.

There was the hay, upon which he had sat. There were changes to contents of the barn from that moment until today. The tarp to which he had crawled had been moved and crumpled in a heap… perhaps by the detectives. One wall close to the hay had fallen outward as if the barn itself had mourned and been grieved in it's seasoned, wooden spirit. His blood stained Cub Scouts bandana, which was tied around his bicep the morning I found him, lay discarded near a box of antique Coke bottles.

I again appreciated the expanse of space that he had crawled from the hay to where I had found him.

There was a barn timber next to the splatter and the remnants of a pool of my sweet child's blood. I looked on the gray beam and saw two tiny marks. Upon that timber, as if painted purposefully and promised to stain forever... were two finger smears from my child's hand, reaching, in what I can only assume was an effort to stand up after shooting himself. They were the beginning of my son's journey toward his New Life.

After the demon and the bullet could not defeat him...he decided… <u>he DECIDED</u> to cry out, to plead to change his mind. God had exchanged his sight for the sinister things Pagiel had chosen. Those two tiny marks are bigger and braver than anything I have ever seen. They were the prelude to his surrender, his war paint drawn in desperation upon a former tree, his signature agreeing to be the great man that he will become.

My son did not die that morning and all that lovely old barn gracefully keeps in it's memory box are now just that... memories. They do not shock or hold me. They, in fact, have helped to release me. Barn cats have since been born there; I was actually careful to step on the hay as some sweet little just-born thing may be sleeping there.

Winter has come and gone, spring awakens all about… unaware of the morning of October 8th.

God gives us Life and we absolutely do not own or control it. My son's decision to choose that barn and to choose to end his life was actually not up to him at all. Very few people are wearing scars of an entrance and exit wound on their temples, very few people make their way in this world WITH sight...let alone 10 feet without it, newly removed.

The entire reason I tell my life story is to help you

understand my son's. To show you, the reader, that it is absolutely not the demon or the bullet that determines your life...but God and his ultimate sacrifice of His son. For you see, in a little, tiny way, I understand what it is to see your son sacrificed. And I am forever changed by two tiny marks of blood on a felled tree that led me back to the blood stained cross made of a different tree 2,000 years prior.

THE
DREAM
OF
REMEMBRANCES

By: Bethany

I told Pagiel I wished he remembered the incident, he said, "I did have a dream about it." I asked him to tell me, which he did freely due to the meds.

This particular day, Pagiel spoke from the morning he opened his eyes until close to midnight. I actually was not aware that they had given him the medicine normally used for narcolepsy until I asked the nurse about his behavior and if it was TBI related. It was the weekend and no changes would be made.

His "dream" seems to me a muddled and foggy recollection mixed with God's protective art of vision after the bullet entered. He remembers getting the gun but not from the location where it actually was. He recalled the place he sat and the last thing... (I truly realize as I am writing this... that he will never see again see this place unless he is granted sight from God). He will never again see the view from the barn and the rain, light and cool; he will never see the hay surrounding a 14-year-old human who had decided this was the absolute most he could bear; he will never see the gun and the morning beckoning for a new day that he decided should be his very last.

He said the first pull of the trigger did not work. That the gun made a clicking noise but did not engage and there was a small dent in the bullet. He told me that he had practiced holding the barrel at the correct angle so that he did not survive to be sent to a psychiatric hospital for being insane.

After examining the firing issue, he closed the revolver and went for another try. The "memory" then switched to a series of clicks that resulted in everything being fine. He went into a place of comfort, bright light and solace. Though he was never in a coma, he has no memory of his original hospital experience or any pain.

What broke my child's heart? Who? When did the problems begin? Some things I simply refuse to write as he will tell them in his own time. I can tell you how I broke his heart.

I was an abused child. I came from a home of horrible, sinister things. This is a novel in itself and, if your mind can imagine it, it happened.

I was unable to have children as a result of some of these things. When I was 26 years old, I went to the doctor as I was absolutely positive I had stomach cancer or Crohn's disease. I chose the restaurant industry as a career when I left home at 14 years old and found that it was a fantastic way to make a lot of money and I loved everything about the culinary world. My ex-husband and I were working doubles almost every day helping a restaurateur in his venture to turn an old ice cream parlor into a true dining facility. I was very sick, emotional and even my bones hurt!

The physician I chose was a woman with a new practice. She asked if I could be pregnant and of course, I told her, "No." It was impossible. She replied that she would not charge me for the visit and to go home to take a pregnancy test in the morning. Pagiel's father quietly said he had one hiding in our bathroom. I was offended! I was actually hurt and scared as I did not want to be hopeful or think of the possibility that I could ever be gifted with a child. We agreed and left.

That evening, in my bed… my mind began to reel. This could not be true! I became afraid… I reached into my nightstand to grab my new Bible. I had in the past year tried to become closer to God though felt entirely unworthy. My mom had given me a burgundy Bible with my name embossed in gold print as many Southern readers will recognize in their mind's eye. I opened it with the quick prayer of, "Give me a sign" and there was his name. As if it was written in bold print. "PAGIEL"

I knew I was pregnant and he was a boy. I told

his father this. I took multiple tests in the morning that the line displaying "Pregnant" showed before the "test" line. After going to the doctor for prenatal care, I found out I was 17-and-a-half-weeks.

My world seemed perfect. It was soon turned upside down with the betrayal of my husband and my best friend throughout my life having an affair. I accept a great amount of responsibility in this affair but it did not ease the pain of the thing itself. Regardless of all the hard stuff, I was honored to bring Pagiel Augustus Griffith into the world on October 18th, 2002 at 9:23 a.m. with very little effort on my part. He had the most amazing eyes, already looking about the room, taking in every detail. Perhaps he knew he should begin making visual imprints immediately. He held his head up independently as well. He was strong and beautiful and perfect. And bore a birthmark of a "P" on his thigh.

I never suffered from postpartum. I was simply ready to show him all the amazing things in life. I felt as natural as anyone could, as if I had been waiting on him to arrive my whole life. Imagine holding a sign at the airport waiting on your best friend to arrive so that the two of you might embark on a grand adventure. This is close to how I can best explain how I felt as a new mom.

THE
CARE
PACKAGE

By: Bethany

While in the hospital as in the nature of these events… many people reached out. I was not sharing Pagiel's story at this time at all. The ones who knew it were very close to us. (We do share freely now but we only began a little at a time.)

A year prior to this, I was to be married to a wonderful man named John. As we were both utterly lost in life, we had no idea how to properly love one another. With bags packed full of previous failed relationships, we chickened out. We did not understand at that time it was the bags we were clutching instead of learning to truly love one another. Our relationship ended and it was sad for all of us.

I received an email from John while Pagiel was in the rehabilitation center. I thanked him. I told him very bluntly Pagiel had shot himself. I had no reason for doing this. Maybe I was tired of telling the entire story just to get to the point. Maybe I felt most comfortable just saying it with John. Maybe I was being cold. I just am not sure. I didn't feel angry at our break-up though I know I was in one of those tightly packed bags I held so dear.

He asked if he could send a care package. I agreed.

This box that came was simple and beautiful. I set them down as I took off the packing tape and begin to go through the contents. It was as if every piece I pulled out melted away the protective ice that surrounded my heart. There was a handmade prayer blanket from John's church, a Superman shirt for Pagiel, homemade beef jerky (a favorite of my son's), chapstick, which I am hopelessly addicted to, inspirational books and a journal that included a picture of toddler Pagiel and me and a pressed four-leaf clover (the little extra leafed, elusive edible plant I can never find on my own). Therein contained not only gifts that one could only give if they knew us, but also gifts that spoke of a future together.

John asked to visit. I was nervous and spoke to Pagiel about it. His heart, too, had been warmed by the care package and he was excited to visit with John.

Now, a little over a year later, we are a family united and we learn to walk by Faith and Love each day. We are the Leigh-Griffith Family with two parents who love not only one another but love our children's other parents and our three children with all of our hearts. This family and covenant of mar-riage teaches us not only to walk with Jesus, but to show the love of Christ as we parent our children better and serve God in our work wherever He sends us.

THE
DAY
OF
RESTORATION

By: Bethany

God had been urging me to talk to Pagiel to see if he remembered anything leading up to his attempt. We had a big chunk of time in the car, so here is our day.

Pagiel began with a memory of sitting on his bed with a demonic voice telling him to kill himself, that the desire of his heart would meet him in heaven. He replied that he didn't know where the gun was; that he didn't want me to have to clean up the mess; that leaving out of the house would wake me. The demon told him where the gun was and to go out the window. He remembered his sight had been very hazy for a bit but the memories of this night are very dark. He recalled the feel of the gun, the weight of it awkward as he climbed over the gate at the barn.

We spoke of the weeks leading up to his breakdown. There were memories that were true and some that were not. As he spoke, he realized the hidden truth. He thought I used to glare angrily at him and growl that he was an evil demon. I never did that, I was so far from God that I saw teenage angst at the time and did not realize the Spiritual Warfare occurring at all. As he was speaking, the Holy Spirit showed him the face of evil that was truly in his memory. The face was contorted and evil, and was not mine.

The demons took forms of two people as well just to speak to him. One was Mark, who wore white and seemed good but told Pagiel to do bad things. The other was David who wore black and told my son how horrible he was daily.

He had watched episodes of Mr. Robot about a young man who struggled with Schizophrenia. He transformed into this boy. The demons encouraged him to dress like Elliot, the main character. To create his own solitude inside a hoodie. They told Pagiel he was Schizophrenic too. Which was a safe thing to believe, the possession would have never been dealt with.

I remember seeing my child's face change. He became gaunt, his eyes appeared lifeless, and he would gag when he tried to eat. I had given him time to mourn over the loss of the desire of his heart so I assumed he would heal.

The devil was working in my life as well, to cause me to be comfortable in this chaos. I refused to see the Truth. He (Pagiel) was becoming completely possessed and taken over by the dark spirits at this point. He was told that he would become all powerful; he was being whispered to about necromancy; he would scream at himself in the mirror that he was disgusting and full of demons and he was weak for allowing it. He followed the Demon Violinist, he was all in.

The demons led him on a journey that would lead him into a barn. He believed everyone hated him… and he, in turn, truly hated everyone. Until today, he still thought a lot of his memories were real.

He said that he took all the bullets out but put them back in; he was nervous but he believed the voices he was hearing was God. He pulled the trigger. He then saw headlights peeking through the wooden walls of the barn, which of course was a vision of his brain going into healing mode. He could see nothing. He did vaguely remember being on the tarp, the feel of it beneath his body.

After our hours-long talk, he was free. He was affectionate for the first time today. Truly affectionate. We held one another, he kissed my cheeks and forehead, we praised Jesus together, we prayed until we were out of breath. He wanted to walk in God's creation; he turned his precious face toward Heaven and yelled, "I LOVE YOU, GOD!!". He lifted his hands and praised his Deliverer and his Soulshine was brighter than his darkness was ever dark.

SINS
OF THE
PARENTS

By: Bethany

Fast forward, almost a year since that terrible and beautiful First Day of Our New Life!

Pagiel is overflowing with Blessings. He is immersed in a world of Music, Fellow Christians and his blind brothers and sisters.

This summer has been a whirlwind of events and an outpouring of love. Pagiel was encouraged from a voice in Japan, our friend, Kojika... to attend camps. He was not so sure about these adventures as he has never been to a summer camp. Now... he has attended three!

Our Pastor who is a beautiful, humble and powerful vessel of God ...was so grateful to speak truth and welcome Pagiel into The Body of Christ. This was a day of Great Healing as all of his family were present. We move from a time when Joseph and I, as his parents, could not speak a civil word to one another and even if we spoke them... we did not mean them. We had great anger in our hearts for one another. Mountains of hurt lived and breathed between us.

The day our son was baptized, the Holy Spirit brought Joseph, his beautiful wife, sweet little brother and wonderful family to church to witness Pagiel entering The Kingdom of God. We all cried as our pastor sprinkled the water and made public that Pagiel belongs to The Father. We hugged and celebrated... together.

My son, whom the Father placed in my care and I did not care for well for a long time... has brought us all to Heaven. Scripture tells us that God is angered for generations because of sin. My beautiful son has come to earth to break this cycle and has been given the Grace to defeat our bondage.

I was reminded of how something like this makes the sins of parents come to light. Tragedy of a child can change your heart; grief and pain are strong encouragers. It is amazing how easy it was to forgive Pagiel's father for every sin he had committed against my son but I held myself rigorously accountable. I audibly spoke forgiveness to his father and stepmother in the emergency room. Of course, forgiving my son was a non-issue. Just in case you were wondering, I have never felt a moment of anger toward my child.

However, I began a great wave of self-therapy with God. I needed to be forgiven. I needed Him to continue to carry me or I would be useless in my son's recovery. I broke open my own chest, dug into my heart and exposed and confessed every ugly thing I had done... ever.

FINAL WORDS FROM MOM

By: Bethany

Pagiel's recovery is a delicate tale to share with others. Of course, the backbone of the process is God. Period. God intervened, as He always does at some point or another in a person's life. The details of Pagiel's journey to find his way to his narrow path did and will differ from yours. But as long as you start with the following things, you will be granted success.

Confess that there is only One God, the God of Heaven above and of earth below; that He sent His son to cover your sins, and spend immense time in Scripture and prayer.

There is an opportunity for us all to choose blessings or curses.   We all go through the very same process of deciding to put God first in our lives and then we are grown by The Holy Spirit. The steps you are given via Scripture and Prayer will be unique to you and will keep you safe, free and loved.

When Pagiel came home from the hospital, he still had a desire for the darkness for a while. Yes, God had rescued him, and he was alive, but that did not mean he was free and safe. God desires to show us the life we can have, and this will take small, steady steps of growth. One would think the miracle of saving Pagiel from the grips of death would be enough, but it usually is not for any of us. We still have a sin nature that keeps our spirit warring with our flesh. Once the "high" of a miracle has passed, our sin nature tells us that we can now do whatever we want, our emotions have leveled out, and maybe God did not perform the miracle at all… it was just a coincidence.

This is why God uses the people he does in Scripture to teach us of our sin (the failure to love God and love others as ourselves… not just the bad things we do or the bad habits we have) and how we can grow *despite* our sin. Sin was not natural for us when we were created, and our spirits long for Our Creator and our intended created selves. The more we sin, the more misery we experience. This is a quick overview of what The Holy Spirit has revealed to us over the past year-and-a-half. The closer we stay to God, and the more we learn of His Holiness, the more we long for the freedom experienced by the death and resurrection of His Son.

Scripture will lead you to the sacraments. Pagiel's baptism was the most beautiful earthly moment of his life. He even emailed a pastor, about baptism, before he attempted, without my knowledge; proof that he was craving salvation in his darkest moments. Our Pastor gives us communion weekly, and that is more powerful than a 12-step program, although those can be necessary for some and I have seen growth through these programs.

But keep focused on our current discussion of Supernatural healing because that is where the true answer lies. (Most 12-step programs are intentionally Biblical as well). God leads us to sacraments in His Word because the Creator of the Universe knows what is best for you. If you make a delicious recipe, you know what ingredients go best in it and would not dare make a cake with salt instead of sugar. This is but a small example of how God knows what is best to make us fully human and fully free.

The Bible is ordained for our understanding and growth. Faith and Love are your medicine, and the Blood of Christ is what shall set you free. How the Holy Spirit leads you, to what church and what recovery path will be between the two of you. But your obedience and sitting beneath truthful leaders and a healthy Kingdom Family are necessary. Knowing that you will grow each day and over time are necessary. Knowing that it will not be easy is essential. But when you reach the day where you no longer dwell in caves of despair, you will realize it was Grace and Mercy that led you there, and you will have joy and contentment as never before.

We spent an unsteady eight months or so diving into Scripture and prayer, and it was strange for us at first. It did not all make sense and Pagiel was not always a willing student. I would have to reach out to other Christians for counsel, pray and drive away dark spiritual attachments. He was rid of two, and his house was clean, but seven more wanted to move in[1]. God wants us to humble ourselves to ask for help, and we did. We stumbled, we asked for God to pick us up and He did. He is Faithful and Unchanging and nothing is too great for Him.

I prayed Ephesians 6:11-18 *(See page 155)* over him every day. He asked me to stop doing it in front of him, so I did it from another room. The power is in the living, breathing Word of God, not in either of us. Keeping your focus on God and the Supernatural Truths will lead you to recovery. There is no other center.

The chapters of your book will be titled differently than Pagiel's, but the author remains the same. He was here before The beginning and will be here for eternity. Will you choose to be with Him or in the book of another?

[1] *Matthew 12:43-45* *(See page 123)*

NOW
WHAT
?

By: David Rush

The question is often asked, what is going on with Pagiel now; what is his life like? The answer to that question is the most exciting part of the story, but also the hardest to put into words.

Pagiel's story is a story of transformation. Over and over, as I've talked with Paigel and his mother, I've asked Pagiel, "What changed?" Meaning, "Why are you not depressed today? Why are you not listening to the same voices you were the day you pulled the trigger? What changed in your life that night?"

Well, the answer isn't that simple. Actually the answer is just one word, but one word doesn't come close to the understanding you are craving. The answer, in short, is God.

You see, Pagiel's life has been transformed by God. That's the only way any life can ever really change. God has to do it; you can't. You can read a thousand self-help books. You can watch videos and go to counseling sessions, but the truth is, there is no real help outside of God's intangible touch. Something has to change, and you can't do it by yourself; only the One who created you can change you.

So, are we without hope? If we don't go to church or believe all that religious stuff, then are we condemned to die? Well, yes and no. Stay with me for a minute. You need to understand one thing; then it will all make sense.

You see, what happened in Pagiel's life is not really any different than the things that happen in all of us. He grew up, separated from truly knowing God. He listened to the wrong voices and, ultimately, tried to self-destruct. So maybe we don't all listen directly to demons who walk among us, but we all listen to the voices of our own making and the voices of our society. Every decision we make, everything we believe about ourselves, everything we think we know, comes from something we've heard or read… someplace.

But were any of those things we heard, were any of those voices the voice of God? Probably not. You see, the first sin of humankind in the Bible is about Adam and Eve who were in the Garden of Eden. The Garden of Eden was a Utopia and they walked and talked with God. But there was another voice- the Bible calls him the Serpent. Now, whether the Serpent was literal or metaphorical doesn't matter, because I'm sure you've met some serpents in your life too - right? Somehow, that Serpent convinced Adam and Eve to take what God hadn't given them. Was it one conversation?

Was it a friendship? Was it merely a whispered voice? We don't know; all we know is they listened.

You and I have the same problem. Nearly everything I know about myself came from voices other than God's. Almost everything I do comes from desires within me that are not from God. Nearly every thought I have about others does not come from God. So, where is God's voice? Well that, my friend, is the right question.

A man named Jesus walked this earth just a few thousand years ago. He was born on this earth, as the Son of God. He was the very embodiment or physical representation of God himself. Jesus said these words: "I am the way, the truth, and the life, no man comes to the Father but by me."

That's a really bold statement!

But isn't that what you and I need? We need to hear the voice of the Father, our Father in Heaven, the Creator of the earth and everything in it, the Creator of you and I. I want to know what He says about me. I want to hear His voice. But I can't - I can't do it on my own.

So how do I get to the Father? Only through Jesus.

How did Pagiel do that? How do I do that?

That's the right question.

"Jesus didn't just come to save us from hell and take us to heaven.

That's not the point.

He came to save us from sin and take us to himself."

-David Rush

THE TREE BRANCH

By: David Rush

After returning home, it wasn't immediately an obvious change. Pagiel was still very disobedient and, honestly still very untrusting of God. Pagiel still missed his old life. His heart had not changed, at least not fully. Only his ability to get what he wanted had changed. Now blind and physically wounded, he couldn't access the Internet or play video games. His world was dark and frustrating.

But, God was still working. Pagiel's life had been spared from the bullet, but God was still working on his heart and mind. I've often found that God's perfect timing is far slower than I would like. I'm sure that's the same for Pagiel. But, God's timing is always perfect, regardless.

A wound cannot property heal instantly. A surgeon cuts deep and the affects are not always visible on the surface of the skin, but the work of the surgeon is no less essential. The same is true of God's work in our hearts. Often the work is deep and not immediately visible on the surface, but is none-the-less essential. That's exactly what was happening in Pagiel's life.

Let's look from another perspective. Remember the words from Jesus in the scripture that Bethany eluded to in a previous chapter? I'll print it here:

"When an unclean spirit [demon] has gone out of a man, he passes through waterless places, seeking rest, and doesn't find it. Then he says, 'I will return into my house from which I came out,' and when he has come back, he finds it empty, swept, and put in order. Then he goes, and takes with himself seven other spirits more evil than he is, and they enter in and dwell there. The last state of that man becomes worse than the first. Even so will it be also to this evil generation."

Pagiel's mind and heart had been emptied, but was dangerously open for another attack. For this reason his mother had begun praying over him daily, and praying for him constantly. She was reading Scripture to him and working constantly with every bit of faith and energy she had to protect Pagiel's "house"... his heart. Pagiel was annoyed by what he thought were her rituals, or what Pagiel called "Catholic ways."

Just an insert... I encourage every parent to do this now, for and with your children, before something terrible happens. Maybe your child will never face the demons that Pagiel did. But every human is attacked by the evils of this world. They desperately need your prayers. They need Scripture. They need to be covered by the protective Spirit of God. In addition, they need a community of people who passionately believe in Jesus, who will willingly and sacrificially give of themselves as the church did for Bethany and Pagiel.

Because of God's perfect timing, and because of Bethany's prayers, something in Pagiel began to change, slowly. There was a war in his soul… there was a war *for* his soul. He wanted to cry out to God, but he also resisted. He knew what it meant to be a Christian, but he couldn't find the courage or strength inside himself. Somehow, he still believed he had to "do" something, and he couldn't "do" it.

Picture in your mind: a child climbing a tree but not knowing how to get down. The child works his way up, then slips and falls to a lower branch, narrowly escaping certain death. The child is screaming and hanging onto a thin, rough tree branch, terrified of the devastating and painful fall below. But under the child is the father, with his arms out, saying, "just let go." The father knows that the fall is only mere inches into his strong arms. But the child is frightened and can only see the distant hard and painful ground. The father waits, unconcerned, knowing that in time the child must let go. The child holds on as long as possible, clawing at the tree bark in a futile attempt to save himself. Finally, having lost all hope, and with his strength drained, the child releases his grip on the branch and falls easily into his father's loving arms.

To continue the analogy in this story, Pagiel spent years climbing dangerously up the tree of his choices. That night in the barn he fell hard onto a lower branch rather than all the way to the ground where he would have died. He got himself into a mess and didn't know how to get down or out of it. The bullet didn't kill him and home was no comfort. He was hanging out on a branch, crying because there seemed to be no hope.

What Pagiel didn't know, or understand, was that his father (God, our heavenly Father) was right beside him, the whole time, waiting for him to stop fighting and just let go.

After returning home to recover, through the turmoil that continued in his mind, Pagiel weakened. Finally, the struggle for his soul was too much and he surrendered. In desperation, in "giving up," he did the only thing he knew to do. One Sunday morning he cried out and let go. He went to the pastor and asked to be baptized.

There's no doubt in my mind, THAT was the moment of Pagiel's salvation. That was the moment he surrendered. I'm also sure he had no idea what that meant. All he knew was he wanted something from God. He let go of the branch and surrendered into his Heavenly Father's arms.

That Sunday morning he was baptized. Pagiel stood and the pastor poured the water over him in baptism. (Many church denominations believe that total immersion is required, but first, because of Pagiel's physical injury, immersing in water was not a good idea and, second, it's not a process used by that particular Christian denomination.)

Pagiel recounted, "At the moment of my baptism it felt as if pure silky gold were being poured over me. I felt like I really felt God there, for the first time.   I wouldn't say that it was the baptism itself that cleansed me, but it was the fact that at that moment I cried out to God for the first time. My heart changed. My desires changed. I wanted to start following God's ways and learning about God".

Those of us who are already saved know this feeling Pagiel describes as the presence of the Holy Spirit; God himself, touching Pagiel. Everyone has a different experience, or feeling, or thought. But there is one thing for sure: when God touches a person, that person changes forever.

"Jesus forgave a thief dangling on a cross, knowing full well that the thief had converted out of plain fear. That thief would never study the Bible, never attend synagogue or church, and never make amends to those he had wronged. He simply said, "Jesus remember me...," and Jesus promised, "Today you will be with me in paradise." It was another shocking reminder that Grace does not depend on what we have done for God, but rather, what God had done for us."

- Philip Yancey

NEW
LIFE

By: David Rush

Something happened in Pagiel's heart at that baptism. Did the baptism change him? No, not specifically. The change was in Pagiel's heart. At that moment, something broke in his heart. He let go of the branch and he fell easily into the waiting hands of a loving father, the hands and presence of God.

The beauty of this story? God met Pagiel's need with open arms! God always does. God will meet you and your needs too. He may not come down on you like liquid gold; He most probably will not. But He will touch your life if you turn to Him, and you will know it.

You see, God did not ask Pagiel to clean up his life and then come to Him. He didn't demand obedience from Pagiel before He would save him. God didn't instruct Pagiel on how to climb back up the tree. God didn't beg and plead and He didn't demand. God simply waited for Pagiel to be ready, really ready, to let go.

And when Pagiel's heart was prepared, when he called out to God, God was there, ready and waiting to pour out all of Himself on Pagiel.

Immediately after the baptism people would ask Pagiel how he felt. "I feel good," was all he could say. "I feel really good."

From that day forward, things began changing in Pagiel's life. Things that he once craved became distasteful to him. The fantasy of the vampire life, having once held a powerful desire inside of him, he now pushed it away, all of it, like one would push away poisonous food.

The Bible went from being a boring book about rules and a demanding God, to quickly becoming a daily hunger in Pagiel's life for his loving Father: God.

Pagiel explained, "What has really, really changed, is that God stepped into my life. I called out for God. I started really crying out for God. I was ready to change. I was ready to say, 'these ways are not doing me any good. It's no good to be calling myself a vampire when I am not. It's no good to think these things about myself. It's no good to sing with the devils'."

Pagiel's attitude or mindset has changed about sin. He once thought, "Ya, I'm sinning, but it's fine. God will forgive me. It's okay. It's no good to say that anymore. Nowadays my mindset is this about sin: Yes, God will forgive me. Yes, I don't need to keep looking over my shoulder and worrying every few minutes about sin. But don't just fall into it. Don't just say it's fine." Pagiel continues, "Now I want God. I don't see God the way I used to.

If you ever meet Pagiel, you will meet a young man whose life reflects the joy he describes. His mind is clear and his voice praises God. His desires for the evil that once consumed him are now a distant memory. His dreams today are to tell everyone he meets about the love of Jesus. He wants to tell you about the true character of God, and about how He saved him. God not only saved his life by moving the gun to just the right spot, but slowly, and purposefully, God saved Pagiel's mind and, more importantly, his soul.

So many things have changed in Pagiel's and Bethany's lives. If you knew them before you wouldn't recognize them today. They're simply different people. God has a way of doing that.

You need to hear about a couple of remarkable things that have happened in the last year since Pagiel tried to kill himself.

GIFT
OF
MUSIC

By: David Rush

Like I said previously, it wasn't easy at first. This is one such story:

Early after his physical recovery and returning home, Pagiel would not sit in the sanctuary at church. He would say it was because the Traumatic Brain Injury made him highly sensitive to noise and the music of worship forced him out of the room.

Pagiel has always loved music and I'm sure the aversion to the worship music was not simply his injury alone, it was also a symptom of that war in his soul.

However, they would come to church, mostly at Bethany's insistence, and the two of them would sit in the Pastor's office until it was time for the sermon.

But one Sunday, a visitor came to Pagiel's church and sang, "How Great Thou Art." Pagiel entered the sanctuary to listen and God worked in his heart.

His heart had been so hard for so many years. But this was the day God began to open additional areas of Pagiel's heart. When she sang, something began to soften inside his soul and Pagiel cried for the first time in 3 years. Pagiel would share that Jesus smiled at him, that day, from the pulpit. With his physical blindness, the woman who sang was not visible to him, but the Spirit that filled her as she sang...was.

In the months that followed, God used music to actually heal Pagiel's sensitivity to sound.

One weekend, a few months later, they were at Victor Wooten Music Camp in Nashville (Wooten Woods), where many beautiful, Spiritual giftings happened. Jonathan Scales Fourchestra was on stage with drums, pan drums and strings. Their music was intense and mathematical…

Bethany noticed a change in Pagiel and asked if something had happened to him. He said, "yes!"

The young men were most likely not Christians but their music was entirely instrumental. God created music, God used His music to cause a physical change in Pagiel's TBI (Traumatic Brain Injury). Minutes later, they called the entire audience of music students on stage. Pagiel stood directly in front of the drummer, who was furiously pounding on his instrument. Pagiel felt no pain, just pure joy.

NEW SIGHT

By: David Rush

Another example:

Remember the chapter, "Give me Sight, if only a Little?" Bethany had told Pagiel that she could not grant him sight but could help him become the best blind guy ever. It is true, none of us can grant sight or breath or even another second of life. But God can... and has.

One day, a few months back, Pagiel prayed for sight, the very next day, he was granted it.

When Pagiel was a little boy, they watched a documentary about, "Bat Boy". It's a true story about a young kid with an exceptional gift no one else had, or so they thought. Bethany said, "I watched this again and again after we were learning all things about blindness. I just kept thinking, 'yes, this kid is amazing but he cannot be the ONLY one.' This led to research and research led to a man named Daniel Kish."

Echo-location was natural for the blind Mr. Kish

as his mother remembers him making noises to navigate his world at 15 months old. Daniel Kish has gone on, in his adult life, to teach the technique of echo-location. In part, because of Pagiel's natural and nearly instant use of echo-location, Daniel Kish is planning to meet Pagiel in the near future.

Bethany and Pagiel delved into everything they could find. Pagiel tried to click, as this is the best noise suggested to create a path of discovery in a world of visual darkness. Their research led them to find out that the visual part of the brain actually begins to work again...but with SOUND! Just as bats figure out in the darkness what to eat and what to avoid in their incredible speed of flight, so can humans create a visual feedback with sound.

In short, the eyes capture reflections and light then sends the light patterns to the brain that interprets the light as tangible images. The same is true of echo-location. Echo-location is the term used to describe this ability to make clicking noises with the tongue that echo or bounce back to the ears, allowing the brain to interpret those sound images and create visible shapes of the world around him.

Pagiel received this gift after praying one night. Normally, learning echolocation takes years of practice and is only successful for a few. But for Pagiel, there was no extensive practicing. There was only a simple teenager's prayer, then there was vision.

Pagiel now "sees" in ways that we can only imagine.

What's even more of a blessing is what Pagiel does not see. His eyes are blind to many of the evils of this world. The pornography that once enraptured his mind and body now has no hold on him. Lust and images, that all boys struggle with, are gone.

But even, more importantly, Pagiel doesn't judge a person on their appearance. He listens with his ears, and with his heart and more importantly with the Spirit of God that lives within his heart. The eyes can be so deceptive for all of us, but now his heart-eyes often see what we can't. And most importantly of all, the best thing he sees is the face of the Holy Spirit. He not only hears the Voice, but can see the face.

A
SIMPLE
SONG

By: David Rush

The first time I met Pagiel, about six months after his attempted suicide, my wife and I sat down on their couch in their trailer house in Georgia. Pagiel was fiddling with his guitar and laughing at his own goofy jokes. We couldn't help but be attracted to his magnetic personality. Then, out of nowhere, he sang a little tune to us and about us.

He made up the words and strummed a few simple cords and my heart melted. My wife was in tears. We couldn't put our fingers on it, but something in his song, or in his spirit, touched a place in our hearts and melted our guards.

Later, I told him a story about a teenage girl whom we have loved since her childhood. She's a girl from a terribly broken home and has suffered unspeakable abuse. She has cried out for love, but has, to date, never believed in the love that has been offered.

I asked Pagiel to imagine she was in a circle of teenagers with him and, even though she would not hear it, to sing her a song, hypothetically.

I have to tell you, even as I write this story, my eyes fill with tears. The love that poured from his spirit for this girl, unknown to him, was nothing less than the heart of God. The words he instantly created were words of compassion and understanding. The notes that flowed from his instrument were cords of light and love. We wept freely as he sang encouragement, love, and tenderness to this girl. I only wish she could have heard it and experienced God's love through his music.

His mother could tell you countless stories of lives that have been touched by him over the past year. Some in small, nearly imperceivable ways, others in ways that have shaken the foundations of the soul for hurting lives.

This is the hand of God. This isn't because Pagiel is especially talented. It's not because he's destined to be a Nashville star. This is only because one day, in a barn in Georgia, Pagiel gave up his life and God salvaged it. It is only because one day, after he was exhausted from the war for his soul, he let go of the branch and fell into the arms of a loving father who has slowly and intentionally molded this young man into a man after His own heart.

These days you'll often see Pagiel in downtown Chattanooga, playing his guitar, telling anyone who will listen how God, on one rainy night, took this blind boy into His arms and saved his life, his mind, and his soul.

Pagiel said to me just recently, "Since then, God has given me so many gifts. Some things He's given me are physical. God gave me a sense of sight through echo-location. God has given me the ability to ride a skateboard. But more than that, I have this peace of mind. I sleep better at night. Better than I ever have. I sleep so much more soundly, so much more softly. It's all because of God. I just love Him."

Today Pagiel can see. His eyes are open. Not physically, but I promise you, if you ever meet Pagiel you will know that he has seen God. You'll want to see what he sees. You will want to know God the way Pagiel knows God.

More importantly, God is calling to you as well. Do you hear Him? Are you listening? Do you recognize His voice? Stop, turn off all the noises of your life. Turn off the voices you've been listening to your whole life. Do you hear Him? I promise, He's calling to you. It's time to let go of the branch.

Pagiel said to me today, while sitting on the couch with a look of praise to God, "That night, I'm not saying what I did was good, but that night God brought good out of it. He took what was defenseless, destroyed, broken, and shattered into millions and billions of pieces, and then He twisted it back. He took what Satan had intended for evil and death and God twisted it back.

"Looking back, what happened was horrible. But, looking back, it makes me smile. It makes me see where God has brought me from that night, how deep in a pit I was. One that I was digging myself into and Satan was helping me dig. God didn't stop Satan and just let me keep digging that pit. No, he stopped Satan and then, over time, he taught me how to refill the pit from the bottom up."

In a recent conversation Pagiel said, "Not too long ago I put a gun to my head and tried to end my life, but God positioned the gun with His personal hands. And now in life, I'm joyful. The only thing I have to deal with today is physical blindness, but I see it as a blessing, to be truthful."

Then with a growing smile on Pagiel's face, he added, "And the first face that I'll get to see, if I never get my sight back in this life, is Jesus Christ, and I can't wait for that day!"

The End
but the story is not over yet

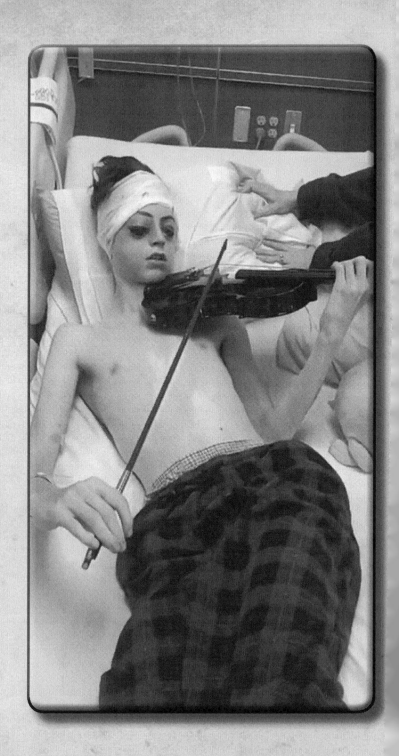

THE EMPTY BEDROOM

By: Bethany

I will never forget the empty bedroom of my child on the morning of October 8th, 2017. It is permanently imprinted into my memory like the ancient carvings one sees upon caves and must only imagine the circumstances surrounding the moment as the carver etched out what mattered most in that time and space. Let me draw you into my cave, my moments, our redemption. Look for a moment with me and align your moments of fear, terror or simply being unsure in your own life. And know there will be a day that you will be as I am now. Full, fulfilled, content and positive I am Loved.

As I went to check on Pagiel, I already knew something was wrong, off, amiss... but put my hand upon the door knob and just walked in. I normally would knock or peek in quietly. His empty bedroom did not shock me. There were no screams or tears or wondering what I should do next. There was only a neat to-do-list of steps that had to be taken. My eyes moved from one part of his room to another. The bed, of course was empty. The window was open. His room was utter chaos as it had been from months of anger, sadness and despair. The window he had broken recently in a fit of rage was the one that whispered his whereabouts. It was the window I leaned upon, peered through and spoke to for answers as I called my boss to let her know I would not make it to work that day, perhaps ever again.

Have you ever seen a scary movie, an older one that relied on psychological horror and suspense instead of gore? This is how the scene went. Flashes of pieces of information met my eyes as my mind tried to keep up with clues and left behind bits of Pagiel.

BAM! Empty bed.

BAM! Open window.

BAM! Laptop, phone, all communication devices present.

BAM! Lack of note from a runaway child.

BAM! Open leather journal to a page written in an alphabet of runic nature I could not decipher.

BAM! The door again as The Holy Spirit told me to leave and go to the barn.

I was far from saved of my own volition. I not only was not calling out to God, I had not wanted anything to do with a God I thought had forsaken me 14 years before when I was soon to give birth to the child I now could not find. In fact, it was I who had forsaken both God and my son. Just as the people of Israel had found themselves in a great sin cycle, so had I. I worshiped other gods, cried out, He rescued me without my repentance and I had a good season of prosperity and rest.

Then, I would fall again. It was not until my son walked boldly to the barn with a .38 revolver to end his life, did I awaken and repent. I did not even fully understand my sin and had passed it down freely to my sweet son.

So here I was, in his empty bedroom with all the things that could have misled me to understand why he shot himself.

Had he died instead of lived, this is how the story could have gone: I would have found his body. I have no idea how long I would have stayed in the barn, looked around, held his lifeless body, cursed God or cried out for Him… eventually, I imagine I would have found the gun. My best friend imagines I would have shot myself as well. I cannot speak to that but if I did not, I would have had to call the police. They would have come to take his body and there would have been an investigation. All the things in his room would have pointed to a mental illness undiagnosed. He would have fallen into a category of suicide statistics that would have led to more confusion about why our loved ones are choosing to end their lives instead of suffering at the reaches and torture of demons.

Please note, I do understand mental illness and there are people who are limited mentally. Most who die from suicide are not. Listen to the attempt survivors and you will hear the stories of voices, urges and a desperation to be rid of them. You will hear stories of sin passed down through abuse, neglect, heart-wrenching tales of parents who were broken and did not love well because they weren't taught to love well. This is wicked and evil, not a mental limitation. There are those who were loved well also. I must speak to those who were loved exceedingly well and still found to be encapsulated in pain from dark places. I realize that we do not have an exact how-to for recovery and, though we may not have your room number and key, I can gladly show you to the hotel with the vacancy sign, give you a GPS address with a path that is narrow but well worth the comfy beds and mints on the pillows. We can even walk with you in a Kingdom journey.

Look around you right now and move your mind to the rest of your home or current living situation. What would someone find and assume if your body were to be at rest today? Would your empty bedroom tell the truth of who you were? Would the pieces of your life, knitted together by detectives assessing your belongings, social media and search history, writings, collections, material objects, pets, children, tales and stories from all that knew you be an accurate description of who you really were? I can tell you that Pagiel, the empathetic and kind human, was very misrepresented by his left-behind things and chapter of life he was in.

Leave a good empty bedroom. There is not nearly enough time to leave a legacy of questions and chaos. Reach out so that you can be healed. It happened here and it can happen where you are right now.

Is Pagiel coming to visit you?

Pagiel's passion is to make himself available to tell others about what Jesus has done in his life.

If you would like to speak with Pagiel or arrange for him to speak to your youth group, school, or other gathering. . . please contact him at Pagiel.Life

"Finally, be strong in the Lord, and in the strength of His might. Put on the whole armor of God, that you may be able to stand against the wiles of the devil. For our wrestling is not against flesh and blood, but against the principalities, against the powers, against the world's rulers of the darkness of this age, and against the spiritual forces of wickedness in the heavenly places.

Therefore put on the whole armor of God, that you may be able to withstand in the evil day, and, having done all, to stand. Stand therefore, having the utility belt of truth buckled around your waist, and having put on the breastplate of righteousness, and having fitted your feet with the preparation of the Good News of peace; above all, taking up the shield of faith, with which you will be able to quench all the fiery darts of the evil one. And take the helmet of salvation, and the sword of the Spirit, which is the word of God; with all prayer and requests, praying at all times in the Spirit, and being watchful to this end in all perseverance and requests for all the saints: on my behalf, that utterance may be given to me in opening my mouth, to make known with boldness the mystery of the Good News, for which I am an ambassador in chains; that in it I may speak boldly, as I ought to speak.

Peace be to the brothers, and love with faith, from God the Father and the Lord Jesus Christ. Grace be with all those who love our Lord Jesus Christ with incorruptible love. Amen."

- From Paul's letter to the church in Ephesus

ABOUT THE AUTHOR

David Rush lives with his wife, Amy, and their little dog, Dixie in southern Ohio.

Dave is the author of a series of Christian books called The Simon Series. The Simon Series is a fictional, yet Biblically factual, adventure series that follow our friend Simon back in time to get to know, personally and sometimes even intimately, the people who formed our history in the Bible.

The stories are filled with action, violence, love, lust, and bloodshed.

Those who read the Simon Series always say the same thing; The Simon books bring our Biblical ancestors to life in a fresh way. Reading the Bible's Old Testament is like reading dry history. It often seems to be a long list of names, times and places that we can't relate to. But the Simon books bring the people to life: dramatic, adventurous, love-filled and violent life.

Grace to you, and peace from God, our Father, and the Lord Jesus Christ. I thank my God whenever I remember you. . . being confident of this very thing, that he who began a good work in you will complete it until the day of Jesus Christ.

Dave has been immeasurably blessed to meet and know Pagiel and his family. "The transformation that God has brought into their lives has challenged me, inspired me and encouraged me in more ways than you can imagine."

Dave and Amy live by the theme of "Tikvah," a Hebrew word meaning "Hope" or "Intense Trust." His intentional walk with God is based on the premise of walking each day in absolute trust - only in the Grace and Mercy of God.

If you would like to connect with Dave and Amy or read more about their lives, go to their personal website at Dave-Amy.com

To get your copy of the Simon Series books, or buy additional copies of the Pagiel book, or for audio downloads go to:

Tikvah.Life

Made in the USA
Columbia, SC
24 June 2019